HTML and CSS
FUNDAMENTALS
Building Blocks of Web Development

Kiet Huynh

Table of Contents

Introduction

Welcome to Web Development

Welcome to the exciting world of web development, where you have the power to create and shape the digital landscape. In this chapter, we'll embark on a journey through the fundamental building blocks of web development: HTML (HyperText Markup Language) and CSS (Cascading Style Sheets).

HTML and CSS are the backbone of the web. They allow you to structure content, define its presentation, and bring your creative visions to life on the internet. Whether you're a complete beginner or have some experience in web development, this book is your guide to mastering these essential technologies.

As we dive into the intricacies of HTML and CSS, you'll learn how to create web pages, format text, add images, and design layouts. We'll start with the basics and progressively explore more advanced concepts, equipping you with the skills to build your own websites and web applications.

Web development is a dynamic and ever-evolving field, and having a strong foundation in HTML and CSS is the first step toward becoming a proficient web developer. So, let's get started on this exciting journey. By the end of this book, you'll have the knowledge and confidence to create stunning web experiences that captivate your audience. Enjoy the learning process and embrace the endless possibilities of web development!

The Importance of HTML and CSS

In today's digital age, the web is an integral part of our lives. From shopping and socializing to seeking information and entertainment, we turn to the internet for almost everything. At the heart of this vast virtual universe are two essential technologies: HTML and CSS. Let's explore why these building blocks of web development are so crucial.

HTML: Structuring the Web

HTML, or HyperText Markup Language, serves as the foundation upon which web content is structured. It provides a standardized way to organize information, turning raw text and media into structured documents. Here's why HTML is of paramount importance:

1. Content Structuring: HTML allows you to define the structure of your web page, from headings and paragraphs to lists and tables. This structural organization ensures that your content is logically arranged and easy to navigate.

2. Accessibility: Properly structured HTML enhances the accessibility of your web content. It makes it possible for assistive technologies like screen readers to interpret and convey the information to individuals with disabilities.

3. Search Engine Optimization (SEO): Search engines rely heavily on HTML to understand the content and context of web pages. Well-structured HTML can significantly improve your site's visibility in search engine results.

4. Cross-Browser Compatibility: HTML provides a common language that browsers understand. Properly written HTML code ensures that your web pages render consistently across different browsers and devices.

CSS: Bringing Style to the Web

While HTML structures content, CSS (Cascading Style Sheets) is responsible for its presentation. Here's why CSS is equally important:

1. Design and Aesthetics: CSS enables you to define the visual style of your web content. You can control colors, fonts, spacing, and layout, allowing you to create visually appealing and user-friendly websites.

2. Consistency: CSS promotes consistency by separating the content (HTML) from its presentation. This means you can update the design of your entire website by making changes to a single CSS file.

3. Responsive Design: With CSS, you can implement responsive design principles, making your web pages adapt gracefully to different screen sizes and devices.

4. Efficiency: By keeping the presentation separate from the content, CSS simplifies the maintenance and scalability of your web projects. It reduces redundancy and makes your code more efficient.

5. User Experience: The design and layout of a website greatly influence the user experience. CSS allows you to create intuitive, visually pleasing interfaces that engage your audience.

In essence, HTML and CSS are the essential tools for anyone looking to create, enhance, or maintain a presence on the web. Whether you're a web developer, designer, blogger, or business owner, a solid understanding of HTML and CSS empowers you to craft compelling online experiences. This book will guide you through these technologies, equipping you with the skills to build beautiful, functional, and accessible websites that make an impact on the digital world.

CHAPTER I
Getting Started

1.1 Understanding the Basics

Before diving into the world of web development, it's essential to grasp the fundamental concepts that underlie the creation of web pages. In this chapter, we'll explore the basic building blocks of web development, providing you with a solid foundation for your journey into HTML and CSS.

1.1 What is Web Development?

Web development refers to the process of creating and maintaining websites or web applications. It involves a combination of skills and technologies to build web pages that can be viewed and interacted with through web browsers. Web development encompasses various aspects, including web design, content creation, server-side scripting, and client-side scripting.

1.2 The Role of HTML

HTML (Hypertext Markup Language) is the backbone of web development. It's a markup language used to structure and present content on the web. HTML documents consist of elements, each serving a specific purpose, such as headings, paragraphs, lists, links, and images. These elements are enclosed in tags, which define their structure and behavior.

1.3 The Power of CSS

CSS (Cascading Style Sheets) complements HTML by controlling the presentation and layout of web content. With CSS, you can define the visual style of your web pages, including fonts, colors, spacing, and positioning. CSS separates content from design, allowing for greater flexibility and consistency in web design.

1.4 The Web Development Workflow

Web development often follows a structured workflow:

- **Planning:** Define the goals and objectives of your website. Plan the site's structure, layout, and content.

- **Design:** Create mockups or wireframes to visualize the site's appearance. Design the user interface and user experience.

- **Development:** Write HTML and CSS code to build the web pages based on your design. Implement functionality using JavaScript or other scripting languages.

- **Testing:** Thoroughly test your website across different browsers and devices to ensure it works as intended. Check for compatibility, responsiveness, and functionality.

- **Deployment:** Publish your website to a web server, making it accessible on the internet.

- **Maintenance:** Continuously update and maintain your website to keep it secure, up to date, and relevant to your audience.

1.5 Your Development Environment

To begin your web development journey, you'll need a development environment. This typically includes a code editor, web browser, and web server (for testing dynamic websites). Popular code editors include Visual Studio Code, Sublime Text, and Atom. Most modern web browsers have built-in developer tools that allow you to inspect and debug web pages.

1.6 Getting Started with HTML and CSS

In the upcoming chapters, you'll learn how to create your first HTML document and structure content using HTML elements. You'll also dive into CSS to style your web pages, bringing your design ideas to life. By the end of this book, you'll have the skills and knowledge needed to build your own websites and explore more advanced web development topics.

Now that we've covered the basics let's move on to setting up your development environment and creating your first HTML document in the next chapters.

1.2 Setting Up Your Development Environment

To embark on your web development journey, it's crucial to establish a robust development environment that will streamline your coding and testing processes. In this section, we'll walk through the steps to set up your development environment, ensuring you have the essential tools at your disposal.

1. Choosing a Code Editor

The first decision you'll need to make is selecting a code editor. Code editors are software applications that facilitate code writing and editing. There are several popular code editors to choose from, and the right one for you largely depends on your preferences. Some well-known code editors include:

- **Visual Studio Code (VS Code):** Developed by Microsoft, VS Code is a free, open-source code editor known for its extensibility, rich features, and strong community support.

- **Sublime Text:** A lightweight, highly customizable code editor that's known for its speed and responsiveness.

- **Atom:** Another open-source code editor with a strong focus on customization and community-created packages.

2. Installing a Web Browser

A web browser is a fundamental tool for web development. It's essential for previewing your web pages and testing their functionality. While most operating systems come with pre-installed browsers, developers often use multiple browsers to ensure cross-compatibility. Popular choices include Google Chrome, Mozilla Firefox, Microsoft Edge, and Safari (for macOS).

3. Utilizing Browser Developer Tools

Modern web browsers come equipped with developer tools that are indispensable for web development. These tools allow you to inspect HTML and CSS, debug JavaScript, monitor network activity, and test your website's responsiveness.

- **Chrome DevTools:** Accessible by right-clicking on a web page and selecting "Inspect" or by pressing `Ctrl+Shift+I` (or `Cmd+Option+I` on macOS).

- **Firefox Developer Tools:** Accessible through the browser menu or by pressing `Ctrl+Shift+I` (or `Cmd+Option+I` on macOS).

- **Edge DevTools:** Similar to Chrome's DevTools, accessible via the browser menu or by pressing `Ctrl+Shift+I` (or `Cmd+Option+I` on macOS).

4. Web Server for Local Development (Optional)

While not always necessary, setting up a local web server can be beneficial if you're working on dynamic websites or web applications. Local web servers like Apache, Nginx, or development-specific servers like Node.js (with Express.js) can help you test server-side code and databases.

5. Version Control (Optional)

Consider using version control software like Git to track changes in your code and collaborate with others more efficiently. Platforms like GitHub and GitLab offer hosting services for Git repositories, making it easier to manage and share your projects.

6. Integrated Development Environments (IDEs) (Optional)

In addition to code editors, some developers prefer using integrated development environments (IDEs) that offer an all-in-one solution for coding, debugging, and project management. Popular IDEs for web development include Visual Studio, JetBrains WebStorm, and Eclipse.

With your development environment set up, you're well-prepared to begin creating your first HTML document, which we'll cover in the next chapter. Whether you choose a code editor or an IDE, familiarity with these tools is essential for a successful web development journey.

1.3 Creating Your First HTML Document

In this section, we will guide you through the process of creating your very first HTML (Hypertext Markup Language) document. HTML is the foundation of web development and is used to structure the content of web pages. By the end of this tutorial, you'll have a basic understanding of HTML and be able to create a simple webpage.

1. Choose a Text Editor

Before you start coding, you'll need a text editor to write your HTML code. You can use any text editor you prefer, such as Notepad (Windows), TextEdit (macOS), Visual Studio Code, Sublime Text, or Atom. These editors provide features like syntax highlighting to make coding easier.

2. Create a New HTML File

Open your chosen text editor and create a new file. To do this, go to "File" > "New" and save the file with an ".html" extension, for example, "index.html." The ".html" extension tells your computer that this is an HTML file.

3. Start with the HTML Structure

Every HTML document starts with a basic structure that includes the `<!DOCTYPE>`, `<html>`, `<head>`, and `<body>` elements. Here's what each of these elements does:

- `<!DOCTYPE html>`: This declaration defines the document type and version of HTML you're using (HTML5, in this case).

- `<html>`: This is the root element that wraps all your HTML content.

- `<head>`: Inside the `<head>` element, you define metadata about your webpage, such as the title and character encoding.

- `<body>`: The actual content of your webpage goes inside the `<body>` element.

Here's an example of the basic HTML structure:

```html
<!DOCTYPE html>
<html>
<head>
   <meta charset="UTF-8">
   <title>Your Page Title</title>
</head>
<body>
   <!-- Your content goes here -->
</body>
</html>
```

4. Add Content to Your Webpage

Inside the `<body>` element, you can add various types of content, including headings, paragraphs, images, and links. Let's add a simple heading and a paragraph:

```html
<!DOCTYPE html>
<html>
<head>
   <meta charset="UTF-8">
   <title>Your Page Title</title>
</head>
<body>
   <h1>Welcome to My First Webpage</h1>
   <p>This is a simple paragraph of text.</p>
</body>
</html>
```

5. Save and View Your Webpage

After adding your content, save the HTML file. Then, open a web browser (such as Chrome, Firefox, or Edge) and drag the HTML file into the browser. You should see your webpage displayed with the heading and paragraph you added.

Congratulations! You've created your first HTML document. While this is a basic example, HTML provides many more elements and attributes to structure and style your web content. In the next sections of this chapter, we'll dive deeper into HTML, covering topics like structuring content and styling with CSS.

1.4 Structuring Content with HTML

In this section, we will delve into the foundational aspects of structuring content using HTML (Hypertext Markup Language). HTML is the fundamental language of the web that allows you to create the structure of your web pages, defining elements and their relationships. By understanding how to structure content with HTML, you'll be able to create well-organized and semantically meaningful web documents.

1. HTML Elements

HTML documents are constructed using various elements, each designed for a specific purpose. Elements are enclosed in angle brackets `< >` and typically come in pairs: an opening tag and a closing tag. The content to be affected by the element is placed between these tags.

For example, the `<p>` element is used for paragraphs:

```html
<p>This is a paragraph.</p>
```

Here's a brief overview of some common HTML elements for structuring content:

- `<h1>` to `<h6>`: Headings of varying levels, with `<h1>` being the highest (most important) and `<h6>` being the lowest.

- `<p>`: Paragraphs of text.

- `<ul>` and `<ol>`: Unordered and ordered lists for items.

- `<li>`: List items inside `<ul>` or `<ol>`.

- `<a>`: Anchor tags for creating hyperlinks.

- `<div>`: A generic container for grouping and styling content.

- `<span>`: A generic inline container for applying styles or scripting.

2. Semantic HTML

Semantic HTML refers to using elements that convey meaning about the structure of your content. For example, instead of using a generic `<div>` for everything, you might use `<header>`, `<nav>`, `<article>`, and `<footer>` elements to describe the sections of your webpage in a more meaningful way.

Semantic elements not only improve accessibility but also assist search engines and developers in understanding the content and its context.

Here's an example of semantic HTML:

```html
<header>
  <h1>Main Title</h1>
  <nav>
```

```html
    <ul>
      <li><a href="#">Home</a></li>
      <li><a href="#">About</a></li>
      <li><a href="#">Contact</a></li>
    </ul>
  </nav>
</header>
<article>
  <h2>Article Title</h2>
  <p>This is the article content.</p>
</article>
<footer>
  &copy; 2023 Your Website
</footer>
```

3. Nesting Elements

HTML elements can be nested inside other elements to create complex structures. It's important to follow proper nesting rules to ensure your document is valid and well-formed.

For example, you can nest a list inside a `<div>`:

```html
<div>
```

```
    <ul>
        <li>Item 1</li>
        <li>Item 2</li>
    </ul>
</div>
```

4. Attributes

Attributes provide additional information about an element and are added within the opening tag. For example, the `href` attribute in an anchor tag defines the link's destination:

```html
<a href="https://www.example.com">Visit Example</a>
```

5. Comments

You can add comments to your HTML code to provide explanations for developers or to temporarily remove code without deleting it:

```html
<!-- This is a comment -->
```

Understanding how to structure content with HTML is the foundation of web development. As you become more familiar with HTML elements, attributes, and semantic structure, you'll be well-equipped to create well-organized web documents. In the next section, we'll explore how to style your content using CSS (Cascading Style Sheets).

1.5 Styling Content with CSS

In this section, we will explore the art of styling web content using CSS (Cascading Style Sheets). CSS is a powerful language that enables you to control the presentation and layout of your HTML elements. It allows you to define how your web page should look, including colors, fonts, spacing, and positioning.

1. Introduction to CSS

CSS is essential for creating visually appealing and user-friendly websites. It separates the content (HTML) from its presentation, making it easier to maintain and update your web pages. With CSS, you can achieve the following:

- Change text and background colors.

- Set fonts and font sizes.

- Adjust margins, paddings, and borders.

- Control the layout of elements, such as centering content.

- Create responsive designs that adapt to different screen sizes.

2. CSS Syntax

CSS rules consist of two main parts: selectors and declarations. A selector identifies the HTML element you want to style, while declarations specify how you want to style it.

Here's a simple CSS rule:

```css
```

```
p {

    color: blue;

    font-size: 16px;

}
```
```

In this example, `p` is the selector targeting all `<p>` elements. The declarations inside the curly braces `{}` define the styles for those elements, setting the text color to blue and the font size to 16 pixels.

## 3. CSS Selectors

CSS provides various types of selectors to target specific elements or groups of elements. Some common selectors include:

- Element selectors: Target all instances of a specific HTML element (e.g., `p`, `h1`, `a`).

- Class selectors: Target elements with a specific class attribute (e.g., `.highlight`).

- ID selectors: Target a single element with a specific ID attribute (e.g., `#header`).

- Descendant selectors: Target elements that are descendants of another element (e.g., `ul li` targets all `<li>` elements within a `<ul>`).

## 4. Cascading and Specificity
```

The "C" in CSS stands for "Cascading," which means that multiple CSS rules can apply to the same element. When conflicts arise, CSS uses specificity and the order of rules to determine which styles to apply. Understanding specificity is crucial for managing complex stylesheets.

5. Box Model

The CSS box model describes how HTML elements are rendered as rectangular boxes. It consists of content, padding, borders, and margins. By adjusting these properties, you can control the size and spacing of elements on your page.

6. CSS Layout

CSS plays a crucial role in controlling the layout of web pages. You can use properties like `display`, `position`, and `float` to create multi-column layouts, responsive designs, and more.

7. External CSS

To keep your HTML and CSS separate and maintainable, it's common to link an external CSS file to your HTML document using the `<link>` element.

```html
<link rel="stylesheet" type="text/css" href="styles.css">
```

This approach allows you to reuse styles across multiple pages and makes updating styles more efficient.

8. CSS Frameworks

CSS frameworks like Bootstrap and Foundation provide pre-designed styles and layout components to streamline web development. They are particularly useful for creating responsive and consistent designs.

Styling your content with CSS is a fundamental skill for web developers. As you become proficient in CSS, you'll gain the ability to transform your HTML documents into visually appealing and well-structured web pages. In the next chapters, we will explore advanced CSS techniques and dive deeper into web development.

CHAPTER II
HTML Fundamentals

2.1 HTML Document Structure

In this section, we will delve into the fundamental structure of HTML (Hypertext Markup Language) documents. HTML serves as the backbone of every web page, defining the content and structure that browsers render as websites. Understanding HTML's core elements is crucial for web development.

1. The Basic HTML Template

An HTML document starts with a basic template, consisting of essential elements:

```html
<!DOCTYPE html>
<html>
<head>
   <title>My Web Page</title>
</head>
<body>
   <!-- Content goes here -->
</body>
</html>
```

```
```

- `<!DOCTYPE html>`: This declaration specifies that the document is written in HTML5, the latest version of HTML.

- `<html>`: The root element that wraps the entire HTML content.

- `<head>`: Contains metadata about the document, such as the page title and links to external resources (CSS, JavaScript).

- `<title>`: Sets the title displayed in the browser's title bar or tab.

- `<body>`: Encloses the main content of the web page, including text, images, links, and more.

2. Elements and Tags

HTML uses elements, represented by tags, to structure content. Tags are enclosed in angle brackets (`<>`). For example, `<p>` is the tag for a paragraph, and `<a>` is used for hyperlinks. Elements are often structured as opening and closing tags, like `<p>...</p>`, with content in between.

3. Headings and Text

HTML provides heading tags (`<h1>` to `<h6>`) for organizing content hierarchically. These tags define the importance of text, with `<h1>` being the highest level and `<h6>` the lowest.

Basic text can be marked up using the `<p>` (paragraph), `<strong>` (strong emphasis), `<em>` (emphasized), and `<span>` (inline container) tags.

4. Lists and Links

HTML supports ordered lists (`<ol>`) and unordered lists (`<ul>`) for structuring content in list form. List items are marked with `<li>` tags.

Hyperlinks are created using the `<a>` (anchor) tag. They can link to other web pages or resources, both within and outside your website.

5. Images and Multimedia

Images are inserted with the `<img>` tag. You specify the image source (URL) and alt text (a description of the image) within the tag.

HTML also supports embedding multimedia content like audio and video using the `<audio>` and `<video>` tags, respectively.

6. Forms and User Input

HTML forms (`<form>`) are used for gathering user input. You can create input fields, radio buttons, checkboxes, and dropdown menus using various form elements (`<input>`, `<select>`, `<textarea>`).

Form submission is typically handled using the `<form>` element's `action` attribute, which specifies where the data should be sent.

Understanding the structure of HTML documents and the usage of essential HTML tags is the foundation of web development. As we progress through this chapter, we will explore each of these aspects in more detail, allowing you to create well-structured web pages.

2.2 Text and Headings

In this section, we will explore the use of text and headings in HTML documents. Textual content is a fundamental component of web pages, and HTML provides various tags to structure and format text as needed.

1. Basic Text Tags

HTML offers several tags for formatting and styling text:

- `<p>`: The paragraph tag is used to create paragraphs of text. It automatically adds space before and after the text, making it a suitable choice for most textual content.

Example:
```html
<p>This is a paragraph of text.</p>
```

- `<strong>` and `<em>`: These tags are used to add semantic meaning to text. `<strong>` indicates strong emphasis (typically displayed as bold), while `<em>` represents emphasized text (typically displayed as italics).

Example:
```html
<p><strong>Important</strong> information goes here, and this is <em>emphasized</em>.</p>
```

- `<br>`: This tag creates a line break within text, allowing you to move content to the next line without starting a new paragraph.

Example:
```html
<p>This text is on the first line.<br>This text is on the second line.</p>
```

2. Headings

Headings are used to structure content hierarchically and indicate the importance of text. HTML provides six levels of headings, from `<h1>` (highest importance) to `<h6>` (lowest importance). Use them appropriately to organize your content.

Example:
```html
<h1>Main Heading (Most Important)</h1>
<h2>Subheading</h2>
<h3>Sub-subheading</h3>
```

- **Semantic Meaning:** Headings also provide semantic meaning to your content, aiding accessibility and search engine optimization (SEO). Search engines use headings to understand the structure of your page.

3. Text Formatting

HTML offers some text formatting tags, although it's recommended to use CSS for styling. Nevertheless, it's essential to know these tags:

- `<strong>` and `<em>`: As mentioned earlier, these tags provide semantic meaning and may also affect text appearance.

- `<u>`: The underline tag is used to underline text. While it may be used for decorative purposes, it's generally not recommended for hyperlink underlines. CSS is preferred for styling.

Example:

```html
<p>This text is <u>underlined</u>.</p>
```

- `<s>` and `<ins>`: The strike-through (`<s>`) and inserted (`<ins>`) tags are used to mark text as deleted or inserted. They may be useful in collaborative editing scenarios.

Example:

```html
<p><s>Deleted</s> <ins>Inserted</ins> text.</p>
```

These HTML tags are the building blocks for structuring and formatting textual content on your web pages. As we progress through this chapter, we will continue to explore other HTML features for creating rich and well-organized content.

2.3 Lists and Links

In this section, we'll delve into lists and links in HTML, two essential components for structuring content and providing navigation within web pages.

1. Lists

HTML offers three types of lists: ordered lists, unordered lists, and definition lists.

- Ordered Lists (`<ol>`): Ordered lists are used for items that have a specific sequence or order. Each list item is automatically numbered.

Example:
```html
<ol>
  <li>First item</li>
  <li>Second item</li>
  <li>Third item</li>
</ol>
```

- Unordered Lists (`<ul>`): Unordered lists are used for items that don't have a specific sequence. Each list item is typically represented with bullet points.

Example:
```html
```

```
<ul>
  <li>Item one</li>
  <li>Item two</li>
  <li>Item three</li>
</ul>
```

- **Definition Lists (`<dl>`):** Definition lists are used to define terms (DT) and provide their definitions (DD).

Example:
```html
<dl>
  <dt>HTML</dt>
  <dd>HyperText Markup Language</dd>
  <dt>CSS</dt>
  <dd>Cascading Style Sheets</dd>
</dl>
```

2. Links

Hyperlinks, or links, are fundamental for navigating between web pages and resources. HTML uses the `<a>` (anchor) element to create links.

- **Basic Link:** A basic link is created using the `<a>` element's `href` attribute, which specifies the URL of the linked resource.

Example:

```html
<a href="https://www.example.com">Visit Example.com</a>
```

- **Internal Links:** Internal links are used to navigate within the same webpage or to other sections of the page. You can use the `id` attribute to target specific elements.

Example:

```html
<p><a href="#section2">Jump to Section 2</a></p>

...

<h2 id="section2">Section 2</h2>
```

- **Linking to Files:** You can link to various types of files, such as images, PDFs, or other web pages, by specifying the file path or URL in the `href` attribute.

Example:

```html
<a href="images/pic.jpg">View Image</a>

<a href="documents/document.pdf">Download PDF</a>
```

- Linking to Email: To create an email link, use the `mailto` scheme in the `href` attribute.

Example:

```html
<a href="mailto:info@example.com">Contact Us</a>
```

- Opening Links in a New Window: To open a link in a new browser window or tab, use the `target` attribute with the value "_blank."

Example:

```html
<a href="https://www.example.com" target="_blank">Visit Example.com</a>
```

Understanding how to create lists and links in HTML is crucial for structuring content and providing user-friendly navigation within your web pages. These are just some of the fundamental features of HTML, and as we progress through this chapter, we'll explore more elements and attributes to enhance your web development skills.

2.4 Images and Multimedia

This section explores the integration of images and multimedia content into your HTML documents, enhancing the visual and interactive aspects of your web pages.

1. Adding Images (`<img>`)

Images play a vital role in web design, making content more engaging and visually appealing. To insert an image into your HTML document, use the `<img>` element. Specify the image's source (URL) using the `src` attribute, along with optional attributes for accessibility and styling.

Example:

```html
<img src="image.jpg" alt="A beautiful sunset" width="400" height="300">
```

- `src`: Specifies the image file's URL.

- `alt`: Provides alternative text for accessibility and SEO.

- `width` and `height`: Define the image's dimensions (in pixels).

2. Responsive Images

To ensure your images adapt to different screen sizes and resolutions, use the `srcset` attribute to provide multiple image sources and let the browser choose the most appropriate one. You can also use the `sizes` attribute to specify image sizes based on viewport width.

Example:

```html
<img srcset="small.jpg 320w, medium.jpg 768w, large.jpg 1200w"

    sizes="(max-width: 600px) 280px, (max-width: 960px) 720px, 1140px"

    src="medium.jpg"

    alt="Responsive image">
```

3. Video and Audio (`<video>` and `<audio>`)

HTML5 introduced native support for embedding video and audio content. You can use the `<video>` and `<audio>` elements to include multimedia files directly into your web pages. Specify the source(s) using the `<source>` element within these tags.

Video Example:

```html
<video controls width="640" height="360">

  <source src="video.mp4" type="video/mp4">

  <source src="video.webm" type="video/webm">

  Your browser does not support the video tag.

</video>
```

Audio Example:

```html
<audio controls>
```

```
<source src="audio.mp3" type="audio/mpeg">

Your browser does not support the audio tag.

</audio>

```

- `controls`: Adds playback controls (play, pause, volume) to the media player.

- `width` and `height` (for `<video>`): Define the player's dimensions.

4. Embedding External Media

You can also embed content from external sources, like YouTube videos or tweets, using iframes or specialized HTML elements provided by the respective platforms.

Example:

```html

<iframe width="560" height="315" src="https://www.youtube.com/embed/VIDEO_ID" frameborder="0" allowfullscreen></iframe>

```

By incorporating images and multimedia elements effectively, you can create visually compelling and interactive web pages that capture your audience's attention and provide a richer user experience. In the next sections, we'll explore forms and user input, allowing you to gather data and interact with your website's visitors.

2.5 Forms and User Input

In this section, we'll dive into the world of HTML forms, which are fundamental for gathering information and enabling user interaction on your website. HTML provides a set of form elements that allow users to input data, such as text, numbers, checkboxes, and more. Let's explore how to create forms and handle user input effectively.

1. Creating a Form (`<form>`)

To create a form, use the `<form>` element. It acts as a container for various input elements. Specify the form's action attribute to define where the data should be sent after submission, typically a server-side script for processing.

Example:

```html
<form action="/submit" method="post">
  <!-- Form elements go here -->
</form>
```

- `action`: Specifies the URL where form data is sent.

- `method`: Defines the HTTP method for sending data (GET or POST).

2. Input Fields (`<input>`)

The `<input>` element is the most versatile form element and allows users to input various types of data. Use the `type` attribute to specify the input's purpose, such as text, email, password, or checkboxes.

Example:

```html
<label for="username">Username:</label>
<input type="text" id="username" name="username" required>
```

- `type`: Specifies the type of input (e.g., text, email, password).

- `id` and `name`: Unique identifiers for the input field.

- `required`: Makes the input field mandatory.

3. Text Areas (`<textarea>`)

For longer text input, like comments or messages, use the `<textarea>` element. You can define the number of rows and columns to control the size of the text area.

Example:

```html
<label for="message">Message:</label>
<textarea id="message" name="message" rows="4" cols="50" required></textarea>
```

4. Radio Buttons and Checkboxes

Radio buttons (`<input type="radio">`) and checkboxes (`<input type="checkbox">`) allow users to select one or multiple options from a list. Use the `name` attribute to group related options.

Example:

```html
<label>Gender:</label>

<input type="radio" id="male" name="gender" value="male" required>

<label for="male">Male</label>

<input type="radio" id="female" name="gender" value="female" required>

<label for="female">Female</label>


<label for="subscribe">Subscribe to newsletter:</label>

<input type="checkbox" id="subscribe" name="subscribe" value="yes">
```

5. Select Menus (`<select>`)

Use the `<select>` element to create dropdown menus. You can define `<option>` elements within it to specify the available choices.

Example:

```html
<label for="country">Country:</label>

<select id="country" name="country">

  <option value="usa">United States</option>
```

```
  <option value="canada">Canada</option>

  <option value="uk">United Kingdom</option>

</select>

```
```

6. Submitting and Resetting Forms

To allow users to submit the form, include a submit button (`<input type="submit">`).
Additionally, you can provide a reset button (`<input type="reset">`) to clear form inputs.

Example:
```html
<input type="submit" value="Submit">

<input type="reset" value="Reset">

```
```

By mastering HTML forms and input elements, you can create interactive web pages that collect
and process user data effectively. In the following chapters, we'll explore more advanced HTML
and CSS concepts to enhance your web development skills.

CHAPTER III
CSS Fundamentals

3.1 CSS Syntax and Selectors

In this chapter, we will delve into the fundamental concepts of Cascading Style Sheets (CSS). CSS is the language used for describing the presentation and layout of web pages, allowing you to control the visual aspects of your HTML content. Understanding CSS syntax and selectors is the first step towards styling your web pages effectively.

1. Linking CSS to HTML

To apply CSS styles to your HTML documents, you need to link your CSS file to your HTML. Use the `<link>` element in the `<head>` section of your HTML document to do this.

```html
<!DOCTYPE html>
<html>
<head>
    <link rel="stylesheet" type="text/css" href="styles.css">
</head>
<body>
    <!-- Your HTML content here -->
</body>
```

```
</html>
```

2. CSS Syntax

CSS rules consist of a selector and a declaration block enclosed in curly braces `{}`. The selector specifies which HTML elements to style, and the declaration block contains one or more property-value pairs.

```css
/* Selector */
p {
  /* Property-value pairs */
  color: blue;
  font-size: 16px;
}
```

3. CSS Selectors

- **Element Selector:** Targets HTML elements by their name.

  Example:
  ```css
  p {
  ```

```
    font-weight: bold;
}
```

- **Class Selector:** Targets elements with a specific class attribute.

Example:
```css
.highlight {
    background-color: yellow;
}
```

- **ID Selector:** Targets a single element with a specific ID attribute.

Example:
```css
#header {
    font-size: 24px;
}
```

- **Universal Selector**: Selects all elements on the page.

Example:

```css
* {
  margin: 0;
  padding: 0;
}
```

4. Combining Selectors

You can combine selectors to target specific elements more precisely.

- **Descendant Selector**: Selects an element that is a descendant of another element.

Example:
```css
article p {
  font-style: italic;
}
```

- **Child Selector:** Selects an element that is a direct child of another element.

Example:
```css
ul > li {
```

```
    list-style-type: square;

}
```


5. Grouping Selectors

You can group multiple selectors together and apply the same styles to all of them.


```css
h1, h2, h3 {
   color: #333;
}
```


Understanding CSS syntax and selectors is crucial for building stylish and visually appealing web pages. In the following sections, we will explore more CSS concepts, including working with colors and text, layout and positioning, responsive design, and CSS transitions and animations.

3.2 Working with Colors and Text

In this section, we will explore the world of colors and text manipulation in CSS. These are fundamental aspects of web design that allow you to control the visual aesthetics of your web pages.

1. Color Properties

CSS provides various ways to specify colors:

- **Color Names**: You can use predefined color names like `red`, `blue`, or `green`.

```css
h1 {
   color: red;
}
```

- **Hexadecimal Values:** You can use hexadecimal values like `#FF5733` to specify colors with precision.

```css
p {
   background-color: #FF5733;
}
```

- RGB Values: RGB (Red, Green, Blue) values allow you to create custom colors.

```css
button {
    background-color: rgb(255, 99, 71); /* This creates a shade of red */
}
```

- RGBA Values: RGBA (Red, Green, Blue, Alpha) values include an alpha channel for transparency.

```css
div {
    background-color: rgba(0, 128, 0, 0.3); /* This creates a semi-transparent green */
}
```

2. Text Properties

- Font Properties: You can set the font family, size, weight, and style for text elements.

```css
p {
    font-family: Arial, sans-serif;
```

```css
  font-size: 18px;

  font-weight: bold;

  font-style: italic;

}
```

- **Text Color:** You can change the color of text using the `color` property.

```css
h2 {

  color: #333;

}
```

- **Text Alignment**: Control the alignment of text within its container using `text-align`.

```css
div {

  text-align: center;

}
```

- **Text Decoration**: Add text decoration like underlines, overlines, or line-throughs.

```css
```

```css
a {
    text-decoration: none;
}

.underline {
    text-decoration: underline;
}
```

- Text Shadows: Create text shadows for added visual effects.

```css
h3 {
    text-shadow: 2px 2px 4px #333;
}
```

Understanding how to work with colors and text in CSS is crucial for designing visually appealing web pages. These properties provide you with the tools to create eye-catching layouts and typography. In the following sections, we will delve into layout and positioning, responsive design, and CSS transitions and animations, further enhancing your web design skills.

3.3 Layout and Positioning

In this section, we will dive into the crucial aspects of layout and positioning in CSS. Understanding how to structure and position elements on a webpage is fundamental to creating effective and visually appealing web designs.

1. Box Model

The CSS box model is a fundamental concept that defines how elements are rendered on a webpage. It consists of the following components:

- **Content:** The actual content of the element, such as text or images.

- **Padding:** The space between the content and the element's border.

- **Border:** The border that surrounds the padding and content.

- **Margin:** The space outside the border, which separates the element from other elements.

By manipulating these properties, you can control the size and spacing of elements on your page.

```css
div {
    width: 200px;
    height: 150px;
    padding: 20px;
```

```
    border: 2px solid #333;

    margin: 10px;

}
```

2. Positioning

CSS offers various methods for positioning elements on a webpage:

- **Static:** Elements are positioned according to the normal flow of the document. This is the default behavior.

- **Relative:** Elements are positioned relative to their normal position in the document flow. You can use properties like `top`, `bottom`, `left`, and `right` to adjust their position.

```css
div {

    position: relative;

    top: 20px;

    left: 30px;

}
```

- **Absolute**: Elements are positioned relative to the nearest positioned ancestor (or the initial containing block if none). They are removed from the normal document flow.

```css
div {
    position: absolute;
    top: 50px;
    left: 50px;
}
```

- **Fixed:** Elements are positioned relative to the viewport. They do not move when the page is scrolled.

```css
div {
    position: fixed;
    top: 0;
    left: 0;
}
```

3. Layout Techniques

- **Floats:** Floating elements allows text and inline elements to wrap around them. This is commonly used for creating multi-column layouts.

```css
```

```css
img {
    float: left;
    margin-right: 20px;
}
```

- **Flexbox:** Flexbox is a powerful layout system that simplifies complex layouts. It allows you to align and distribute space among elements with ease.

```css
.container {
    display: flex;
    justify-content: space-between;
}
```

- **Grid:** CSS Grid Layout provides a two-dimensional grid system for controlling both rows and columns. It's ideal for creating grid-based layouts.

```css
.container {
    display: grid;
    grid-template-columns: 1fr 1fr 1fr;
}
```

Mastering layout and positioning is essential for crafting visually appealing and user-friendly websites. In the following sections, we'll explore responsive design techniques and CSS transitions and animations, enabling you to create modern and dynamic web experiences.

3.4 Responsive Design

In this section, we will explore the concept of responsive design in CSS. With the proliferation of various devices and screen sizes, it's crucial to create websites that adapt and look great on different platforms, from large desktop monitors to small mobile screens.

1. Media Queries

Media queries are a fundamental part of responsive web design. They allow you to apply different styles based on the characteristics of the device or viewport. Typically, media queries are defined in CSS using the `@media` rule.

```css
/* Style for screens with a width of 768 pixels or larger */

@media screen and (min-width: 768px) {

  body {

    font-size: 16px;

  }

}


/* Style for screens with a width of 320 pixels or smaller (e.g., smartphones) */

@media screen and (max-width: 320px) {

  body {

    font-size: 14px;

  }

}
```

```
```

By using media queries, you can adjust typography, layout, and other design elements to provide an optimal viewing experience for various devices.

2. Fluid Layouts

To create responsive layouts, it's essential to use relative units such as percentages and ems for sizing elements instead of fixed pixels. This allows content to adapt and flow smoothly on different screen sizes.

```css
.container {
    width: 80%;
    margin: 0 auto;
}
```

3. Mobile-First Design

A common approach to responsive design is the "mobile-first" strategy. Start by designing for mobile devices and then progressively enhance the layout and features for larger screens using media queries. This ensures a solid foundation for all devices.

4. Flexbox and CSS Grid

Flexbox and CSS Grid Layout are powerful tools for building responsive designs. Flexbox excels at creating flexible and dynamic layouts, while CSS Grid provides precise control over both rows and columns.

```css
/* Using Flexbox for a responsive navigation menu */
.nav-menu {
    display: flex;
    flex-direction: column;
}

/* Using CSS Grid for a responsive grid layout */
.grid-container {
    display: grid;
    grid-template-columns: repeat(auto-fit, minmax(200px, 1fr));
}
```

5. Responsive Images

To optimize image loading and display, use the `max-width: 100%;` rule to ensure images scale proportionally to the width of their container. Additionally, consider using the `srcset` attribute to provide different image sources for different screen resolutions.

```html
<img src="image.jpg" alt="Responsive Image" style="max-width: 100%;">
```

```
```

Responsive design is crucial for providing a seamless user experience across a wide range of devices. By implementing these techniques and principles, you can create websites that adapt gracefully to the diversity of the modern web landscape. In the next section, we'll delve into CSS transitions and animations, adding interactivity and engagement to your web projects.

3.5 CSS Transitions and Animations

This section explores the world of CSS transitions and animations, enabling you to add engaging and dynamic elements to your web pages.

1. CSS Transitions

CSS transitions allow you to smoothly change the property values of elements over a specified duration. This creates a more pleasing user experience by providing visual feedback for actions like hover or click.

Here's an example of a simple hover effect on a button:

```css
/* Define the initial state */
.button {
    background-color: #3498db;
    transition: background-color 0.3s ease;
}

/* Define the hover state */
.button:hover {
    background-color: #2980b9;
}
```

In this case, the background color changes gradually when you hover over the button, thanks to the transition property.

2. CSS Animations

While transitions are ideal for simple animations, CSS animations offer more advanced and complex animation capabilities. Animations are defined using the `@keyframes` rule.

```css
/* Define a basic animation */
@keyframes spin {
    0% { transform: rotate(0deg); }
    100% { transform: rotate(360deg); }
}

/* Apply the animation to an element */
.spinner {
    animation: spin 2s linear infinite;
}
```

This animation example rotates an element continuously when applied to an HTML element with the class "spinner."

3. Transition vs. Animation

Use transitions for simple state changes like hover effects and subtle animations. For more complex and continuous animations, CSS animations are a better choice.

4. Animation Properties

CSS animations offer a wide range of properties to control timing, iteration, and more. Some essential animation properties include `animation-duration`, `animation-timing-function`, `animation-iteration-count`, and `animation-delay`.

5. Browser Compatibility

While CSS transitions and animations are well-supported in modern browsers, it's essential to provide fallbacks or use JavaScript for older browsers when needed.

Adding transitions and animations to your web projects can make them more interactive and visually appealing. By mastering these techniques, you can create engaging user experiences. In the following chapters, we'll explore more advanced topics in web development.

CHAPTER IV
Combining HTML and CSS

4.1 Building Your First Web Page

In this chapter, we'll embark on the journey of creating your first web page by combining HTML and CSS. This practical guide will walk you through the process step by step.

1. HTML Structure

Before diving into CSS, let's start by setting up the basic structure of your web page using HTML. Here's an example:

```html
<!DOCTYPE html>
<html>
<head>
    <title>My First Web Page</title>
</head>
<body>
    <header>
        <h1>Welcome to My Website</h1>
        <nav>
```

```
      <ul>
        <li><a href="#">Home</a></li>
        <li><a href="#">About</a></li>
        <li><a href="#">Contact</a></li>
      </ul>
    </nav>
  </header>
  <main>
    <h2>About Me</h2>
    <p>Hello! I'm a web developer.</p>
  </main>
  <footer>
    <p>&copy; 2023 My Website</p>
  </footer>
</body>
</html>
```

This code sets up a basic HTML structure with a header, navigation, main content, and footer.

2. Adding CSS

Now, let's make your web page visually appealing by adding CSS styles. Create a separate CSS file (e.g., `styles.css`) and link it to your HTML document:

```html
<head>
  <link rel="stylesheet" type="text/css" href="styles.css">
</head>
```

In `styles.css`, you can define styles for various elements. For example, to change the background color of the header:

```css
header {
  background-color: #3498db;
  color: white;
  text-align: center;
  padding: 20px;
}
```

This CSS snippet sets the background color, text color, alignment, and padding for the header.

3. Styling Navigation

You can style navigation menus to create attractive menus. For instance, styling the navigation links as buttons:

```css
nav ul {
    list-style-type: none;
    padding: 0;
    text-align: center;
}

nav li {
    display: inline;
    margin: 0 10px;
}

nav a {
    text-decoration: none;
    padding: 5px 10px;
    background-color: #3498db;
    color: white;
    border-radius: 5px;
}
```

4. Responsive Design

Consider making your web page responsive, ensuring it looks great on various screen sizes. You can use media queries to adjust styles for different devices.

```css
@media (max-width: 768px) {

  /* Styles for smaller screens */

  header {

    font-size: 24px;

  }


  /* Adjust other styles as needed */

}
```

5. Testing and Debugging

Don't forget to test your web page on different browsers and devices to ensure compatibility. Use browser developer tools to debug and fine-tune your styles.

With these fundamental steps, you'll create your first web page, applying HTML and CSS to structure and style it. As you progress, you'll learn more advanced techniques for web development.

4.2 Creating Navigation Menus

In this section, we will explore the process of creating navigation menus for your web page. Navigation menus are a crucial part of any website as they guide users through the content and help them find what they're looking for. We'll cover the HTML and CSS needed to create various types of navigation menus.

1. HTML Structure

First, let's establish the HTML structure for a basic navigation menu. A common approach is to use an unordered list (`<ul>`) with list items (`<li>`) for each menu item and hyperlinks (`<a>`) for the links.

Here's an example HTML structure for a simple horizontal navigation menu:

```html
<nav>
  <ul>
    <li><a href="#">Home</a></li>
    <li><a href="#">About</a></li>
    <li><a href="#">Services</a></li>
    <li><a href="#">Portfolio</a></li>
    <li><a href="#">Contact</a></li>
  </ul>
</nav>
```

2. Basic CSS Styling

Next, let's add some basic CSS styles to make the navigation menu visually appealing. We can style the navigation bar by targeting the `<nav>` element and the list items `<li>`.

```css
nav {
    background-color: #333; /* Background color for the navigation bar */
}

nav ul {
    list-style-type: none; /* Remove bullet points from list items */
    padding: 0; /* Remove default padding */
}

nav li {
    display: inline; /* Display list items horizontally */
    margin-right: 20px; /* Add spacing between menu items */
}

nav a {
    text-decoration: none; /* Remove underline from links */
    color: white; /* Text color for menu items */
    font-weight: bold; /* Make text bold */
```

```
}
```
```

These styles set the background color, remove default list styles, and make the menu items display horizontally with appropriate spacing.

## 3. Dropdown Menus

To create a dropdown menu for subpages or sections, you can nest another `<ul>` inside an `<li>`. Here's an example:

```html
<nav>
  <ul>
    <li><a href="#">Home</a></li>
    <li><a href="#">About</a></li>
    <li>
      <a href="#">Services</a>
      <ul>
        <li><a href="#">Service 1</a></li>
        <li><a href="#">Service 2</a></li>
        <li><a href="#">Service 3</a></li>
      </ul>
    </li>
    <li><a href="#">Portfolio</a></li>
```
```

```
    <li><a href="#">Contact</a></li>
  </ul>
</nav>
```

You can style the dropdown menu with CSS to make it appear when hovering over the parent item.

4. Responsive Navigation

For responsive design, consider using media queries to adjust the navigation menu's appearance on smaller screens, such as collapsing it into a "hamburger" menu.

```css
/* Media query for small screens */
@media (max-width: 768px) {
  nav ul {
    display: none; /* Hide the menu items */
  }

  /* Add a button or icon for the mobile menu */
  .mobile-menu-button {
    display: block;
  }
}
```

```
```

This CSS hides the menu items on small screens and provides a way to toggle the menu's visibility.

By following these steps and customizing the HTML and CSS to fit your website's design, you can create navigation menus that enhance user navigation and improve the overall user experience.

4.3 Styling Forms and Buttons

In this section, we will delve into the art of styling HTML forms and buttons using CSS. Forms are essential for gathering user input, and well-designed buttons can enhance the overall user experience. We'll explore various techniques to style forms and buttons effectively.

1. HTML Forms

Before diving into CSS styling, let's create a basic HTML form structure. HTML forms consist of input elements like text fields, checkboxes, radio buttons, and submit buttons. Here's an example of a simple contact form:

```html
<form>
    <label for="name">Name:</label>
    <input type="text" id="name" name="name" placeholder="Your name" required>

    <label for="email">Email:</label>
    <input type="email" id="email" name="email" placeholder="Your email" required>

    <label for="message">Message:</label>
    <textarea id="message" name="message" placeholder="Your message" rows="4" required></textarea>

    <input type="submit" value="Submit">
</form>
```

```
```

2. Basic CSS Styling

To style the form elements, we can target them using CSS selectors. Here's an example of basic CSS styles to improve the form's appearance:

```css
form {
    width: 300px;
    margin: 0 auto;
}

label {
    display: block;
    margin-bottom: 10px;
}

input[type="text"],
input[type="email"],
textarea {
    width: 100%;
    padding: 10px;
    margin-bottom: 15px;
    border: 1px solid #ccc;
```

```css
    border-radius: 5px;

    font-size: 16px;

}


input[type="submit"] {

    background-color: #007BFF;

    color: white;

    padding: 10px 20px;

    border: none;

    border-radius: 5px;

    font-size: 16px;

    cursor: pointer;

}


input[type="submit"]:hover {

    background-color: #0056b3;

}
```

These styles set the form's width, provide spacing for labels, style text fields and textareas, and create an attractive submit button with a hover effect.

3. Advanced Styling

For more advanced styling, you can explore CSS frameworks like Bootstrap, which offer pre-designed form components and buttons. These frameworks provide a consistent and responsive design, making it easier to create professional-looking forms and buttons.

4. Customization

To customize the appearance further, you can use CSS to modify colors, fonts, and dimensions according to your website's design guidelines. Always ensure that your forms are user-friendly and accessible, with clear labels and proper validation messages.

By following these steps and tailoring the CSS to match your project's design requirements, you'll be able to create visually appealing forms and buttons that enhance the user experience on your website.

4.4 Building a Simple Portfolio

In this section, we'll take you through the process of creating a basic portfolio webpage by combining HTML and CSS. A portfolio website is an excellent way to showcase your work, projects, or personal achievements. By the end of this chapter, you'll have a functional and visually appealing portfolio webpage.

1. HTML Structure

First, let's outline the HTML structure of our portfolio webpage. We'll create a simple layout consisting of a header, a section for project entries, and a footer. Here's an example structure:

```html
<!DOCTYPE html>
<html lang="en">
<head>
    <meta charset="UTF-8">
    <meta name="viewport" content="width=device-width, initial-scale=1.0">
    <link rel="stylesheet" href="styles.css">
    <title>My Portfolio</title>
</head>
<body>
    <header>
        <h1>My Portfolio</h1>
        <p>Welcome to my portfolio website.</p>
    </header>
```

```
  <section id="projects">

    <!-- Project entries will go here -->

  </section>

  <footer>

    <p>&copy; 2023 My Portfolio</p>

  </footer>

</body>

</html>
```

2. CSS Styling

Next, let's style our portfolio webpage using CSS. You can create a separate `styles.css` file and link it in the HTML's `<head>` section. Below are some basic styles to get you started:

```css
/* Reset some default styles */
body, h1, p {
  margin: 0;
  padding: 0;
}

/* Style the header */
header {
  background-color: #007BFF;
```

```css
    color: white;

    text-align: center;

    padding: 40px 0;

}


/* Style the project section */

#projects {

    max-width: 800px;

    margin: 0 auto;

    padding: 20px;

}


/* Style the footer */

footer {

    background-color: #f2f2f2;

    text-align: center;

    padding: 10px 0;

}
```
```

## 3. Adding Project Entries

Inside the `#projects` section, you can add individual project entries. Each entry can consist of an image, a project title, a brief description, and links to view more details or the project itself. Here's a simplified example:
```

```html
<article class="project">

    <img src="project1.jpg" alt="Project 1">

    <h2>Project 1</h2>

    <p>A brief description of project 1.</p>

    <a href="#">Learn More</a>

</article>
```

You can replicate this structure for multiple project entries.

4. Further Customization

To make your portfolio truly unique, you can customize the CSS styles, add animations, and use JavaScript to enhance interactivity if desired. Additionally, consider using CSS frameworks or libraries like Bootstrap or Font Awesome for additional styling and icons.

By following these steps, you'll have the foundation of a simple portfolio webpage. Feel free to expand and personalize it to showcase your own projects, achievements, and personality on the web.

CHAPTER V
Advanced HTML and CSS

5.1 Semantic HTML Elements

In this section, we'll delve into the importance of semantic HTML elements in web development. Semantic elements play a crucial role in structuring web content, enhancing accessibility, and improving search engine optimization (SEO). Let's explore semantic HTML elements and learn how to use them effectively.

1. What Are Semantic Elements?

Semantic HTML elements are tags that carry meaning about the structure and content of a web page. Unlike non-semantic elements like `<div>` and `<span>`, which are used primarily for styling and layout purposes, semantic elements provide context and clarity to both browsers and developers.

2. Common Semantic Elements

Here are some common semantic HTML5 elements:

- `<header>`: Represents a container for introductory content or a set of navigational links.

- `<nav>`: Defines a section containing navigation links.

- `<main>`: Represents the main content of a document and is unique to the document.

- `<article>`: Represents a self-contained composition, such as a blog post or news article.

- `<section>`: Defines a standalone section of content within a document.

- `<aside>`: Represents content that is tangentially related to the content around it, often placed in sidebars.

- `<footer>`: Represents a container for footer content, such as copyright information.

3. Benefits of Semantic Elements

Using semantic elements offers several advantages:

- **Accessibility**: Semantic elements provide meaningful structure for screen readers, making your website more accessible to users with disabilities.

- **SEO:** Search engines can better understand the content and hierarchy of your page, potentially improving search rankings.

- **Maintenance:** Semantic code is easier to read and maintain, benefiting developers working on the project.

- **Clarity:** Semantic elements make the purpose of each section clear in the HTML, aiding collaboration among developers.

4. Examples of Usage

Let's see some examples of how to use semantic elements in HTML:

```html
<header>
   <h1>Welcome to Our Website</h1>
</header>
```

```
<nav>
  <ul>
    <li><a href="/">Home</a></li>
    <li><a href="/about">About</a></li>
    <li><a href="/contact">Contact</a></li>
  </ul>
</nav>

<main>
  <article>
    <h2>Article Title</h2>
    <p>Content of the article...</p>
  </article>
</main>

<aside>
  <h3>Related Links</h3>
  <ul>
    <li><a href="/news">Latest News</a></li>
    <li><a href="/events">Upcoming Events</a></li>
  </ul>
</aside>

<footer>
  <p>&copy; 2023 Your Website</p>
```

```
</footer>
```

5. Best Practices

- Use semantic elements whenever possible to structure your content.

- Combine semantic elements appropriately to create a well-organized document.

- Ensure that the content within semantic elements accurately reflects their purpose.

By incorporating semantic HTML elements into your web projects, you'll not only improve the quality and accessibility of your websites but also enhance the overall user experience and search engine visibility.

5.2 Flexbox and Grid Layouts

In this section, we will explore two powerful layout systems in CSS: Flexbox and Grid. These layout techniques have revolutionized the way we design web pages by providing efficient and flexible ways to create complex layouts.

1. Introduction to Flexbox and Grid

- **Flexbox (Flexible Box):** Flexbox is designed for arranging elements in a one-dimensional space, either horizontally or vertically. It simplifies tasks like distributing space among items in an even or dynamic manner and aligning items within a container.

- **Grid Layout:** Grid Layout, often referred to as CSS Grid, is a two-dimensional system that enables you to create grid-based layouts. You can define rows and columns to create complex, responsive designs with precision.

2. Flexbox

Key Concepts:

- **Flex Container:** The parent element with `display: flex` or `display: inline-flex`.

- **Flex Items:** The children of a flex container.

- **Main Axis and Cross Axis:** The main axis is defined by the `flex-direction`, and the cross axis is perpendicular to it.

- **Flex Properties:** You can control the layout using properties like `flex-grow`, `flex-shrink`, and `flex-basis`.

Example:

```css
.container {
    display: flex;
    flex-direction: row; /* or column */
    justify-content: center; /* align items horizontally */
    align-items: center; /* align items vertically */
}
```

3. Grid Layout

Key Concepts:

- **Grid Container:** The parent element with `display: grid`.

- **Grid Items:** The children of a grid container.

- **Grid Rows and Columns:** You can define rows and columns using properties like `grid-template-rows` and `grid-template-columns`.

- **Grid Gaps:** Control the space between grid items with `grid-row-gap` and `grid-column-gap`.

Example:

```css
.container {
    display: grid;
    grid-template-columns: 1fr 2fr 1fr; /* Three columns with different widths */
    grid-gap: 10px; /* Space between items */
}
```

4. When to Use Flexbox and Grid

- Use Flexbox for arranging items in a single dimension, like a navigation bar or a row of buttons.

- Use Grid Layout for creating two-dimensional layouts, such as complex grids of articles or product listings.

- Often, you can combine both techniques to achieve sophisticated layouts.

5. Browser Support

Both Flexbox and Grid Layout have good browser support in modern browsers. However, always consider the target audience and browser compatibility when using advanced CSS features.

6. Best Practices

- Plan your layout before implementing Flexbox or Grid.

- Use meaningful class names and comments in your CSS for better maintainability.

- Test your layouts on various screen sizes to ensure responsiveness.

By mastering Flexbox and Grid Layout, you'll have powerful tools at your disposal to create visually appealing and responsive web designs. These layout systems are essential skills for any web developer looking to build modern, flexible web pages.

5.3 CSS Variables

CSS Variables, also known as Custom Properties, are a powerful feature in modern CSS that allows you to define reusable values in your stylesheets. They provide a way to store and reuse values such as colors, fonts, and spacing throughout your CSS code. This results in more maintainable, flexible, and consistent styles for your web projects.

1. Declaration and Usage of CSS Variables

To declare a CSS variable, use the `--` prefix followed by a name for your variable:

```css
:root {
  --main-bg-color: #3498db;
  --font-family: Arial, sans-serif;
  --spacing-unit: 8px;
}
```

You can then use these variables in your CSS rules:

```css
body {
  background-color: var(--main-bg-color);
```

```
  font-family: var(--font-family);

  margin: var(--spacing-unit);

  padding: calc(2 * var(--spacing-unit));

}
```

2. Scope of CSS Variables

CSS variables are scoped, which means they are accessible within the element where they are defined and its descendants. They follow the cascade and inheritence rules of CSS, making them flexible and easy to override when needed.

3. Dynamic Value Changes

One of the key advantages of CSS variables is that you can change their values dynamically using JavaScript. This enables you to create themes, respond to user interactions, or adapt to different device sizes without modifying your CSS files.

```javascript
// JavaScript code to change the background color dynamically

document.documentElement.style.setProperty('--main-bg-color', 'red');
```

4. Fallback Values

You can provide fallback values for CSS variables, ensuring that your styles remain functional even if the variable is undefined or unsupported in older browsers:

```css
body {
  background-color: var(--main-bg-color, #3498db); /* Fallback to #3498db if variable is undefined */
}
```

5. Use Cases

- **Consistent Theming:** CSS variables make it easier to maintain a consistent design theme across your website by centralizing color, typography, and spacing definitions.

- **Responsive Design:** You can adjust variable values based on screen size or device type, simplifying responsive design.

- **Dark Mode:** CSS variables are commonly used to implement dark mode themes that users can toggle on or off.

- **Accessibility:** Variables can store values for things like font size and line height, making it simple to adjust these values for better accessibility.

- **Code Maintainability:** By reducing repetition of values, your code becomes more maintainable and easier to update.

6. Browser Support

CSS variables have good support in modern browsers, including Chrome, Firefox, Safari, and Edge. However, older versions of Internet Explorer (IE) do not support them, so be sure to consider your target audience when using CSS variables.

By incorporating CSS variables into your web development workflow, you can create more flexible and maintainable stylesheets that adapt to changing requirements and design trends.

5.4 Custom Fonts and Icons

In modern web design, custom fonts and icons play a crucial role in creating unique and visually appealing websites. This chapter explores how to incorporate custom fonts and icons into your HTML and CSS to enhance the typography and iconography of your web projects.

1. Using Custom Fonts

Custom fonts allow you to move beyond the standard web-safe fonts like Arial and Times New Roman. You can choose from a vast library of fonts available on the web or even use your own custom font files. Here's how to get started:

a. Font Services

Many font services, such as Google Fonts and Adobe Fonts, provide a wide selection of fonts that you can easily integrate into your website. Here's a basic example of how to include a Google Font in your HTML:

```html
<link href="https://fonts.googleapis.com/css2?family=Roboto:wght@400;700&display=swap" rel="stylesheet">
```

Then, apply the custom font to your CSS styles:

```css
```

```css
body {
  font-family: 'Roboto', sans-serif;
}
```

b. Self-Hosted Fonts

If you have custom font files (e.g., .woff or .ttf), you can host them on your server and include them in your CSS using `@font-face`:

```css
@font-face {
  font-family: 'CustomFont';
  src: url('path/to/custom-font.woff') format('woff');
  font-weight: normal;
  font-style: normal;
}

body {
  font-family: 'CustomFont', sans-serif;
}
```

2. Working with Icon Fonts

Icon fonts are a popular way to add scalable vector icons to your web projects. They are essentially fonts where each character is an icon. FontAwesome and Ionicons are well-known icon font libraries. Here's how to use them:

a. Linking to Icon Fonts

Include the icon font library's stylesheet in your HTML:

```html
<link rel="stylesheet" href="https://cdnjs.cloudflare.com/ajax/libs/font-awesome/6.0.0-beta3/css/all.min.css">
```

b. Adding Icons

To add an icon, use HTML elements like `<i>` or `<span>` with appropriate class names:

```html
<i class="fas fa-heart"></i> <!-- FontAwesome heart icon -->
```

3. Scalability and Styling

One of the key advantages of using icon fonts is their scalability and ease of styling. You can change their size, color, and other properties just like regular text.

4. Considerations

When using custom fonts and icon fonts, consider the following:

- **Performance:** Loading custom fonts can impact page load times. Use font subsets to include only the characters you need and consider font-display options to manage font rendering.

- **Accessibility:** Ensure that your chosen fonts are legible and accessible to all users, including those with disabilities.

- **Licensing:** Be aware of font licensing restrictions, especially when using custom fonts. Some fonts may require a license for commercial use.

- **Fallbacks:** Always provide fallback font choices in case the custom font fails to load.

By incorporating custom fonts and icons into your web development projects, you can elevate the visual appeal and user experience of your websites. Whether you're aiming for a unique typography style or need to use specific icons for your interface elements, these techniques will help you achieve your design goals.

CHAPTER VI
Web Development Tools

6.1 Code Editors and Integrated Development Environments (IDEs)

Choosing the right code editor or integrated development environment (IDE) is a critical decision for web developers. These tools significantly impact your coding efficiency and overall development experience. In this section, we'll explore various code editors and IDEs commonly used in web development and provide insights into how to select the best one for your needs.

1. Code Editors

Code editors are lightweight, text-focused tools designed primarily for writing and editing code. They are minimalistic, fast, and highly customizable. Here are some popular code editors:

a. Visual Studio Code (VS Code)

Visual Studio Code is a free, open-source code editor developed by Microsoft. It offers a wide range of extensions, making it suitable for various programming languages, including HTML, CSS, JavaScript, and more. VS Code's features include intelligent code completion, debugging, and Git integration.

b. Sublime Text

Sublime Text is a lightweight, highly customizable code editor. It's known for its speed and smooth performance. It supports multiple selections, a powerful find-and-replace feature, and an extensive package ecosystem for added functionality.

c. Atom

Atom is another open-source, hackable code editor created by GitHub. It is known for its user-friendly interface and ease of customization. Atom provides a package manager for extending functionality, and it's a great choice for web developers.

d. Notepad++

Notepad++ is a free, Windows-exclusive code editor that's simple and fast. While not as feature-rich as some other editors, it's excellent for quick edits and small tasks.

2. Integrated Development Environments (IDEs)

IDEs are more comprehensive tools that integrate various features into a single environment. They often include code editors, debugging tools, build systems, and more. Here are a few notable web development IDEs:

a. Visual Studio

Visual Studio is a powerful IDE developed by Microsoft. It's known for its robust features, including integrated debugging, code analysis, and support for a wide range of programming languages. Visual Studio offers different editions, with the Community edition being free for individual developers.

b. WebStorm

WebStorm is a commercial IDE specifically designed for web development. It offers advanced coding assistance, intelligent navigation, and support for popular web technologies like React, Angular, and Vue.js. WebStorm's live preview and debugging capabilities make it a favorite among web developers.

c. PhpStorm

PhpStorm is an IDE tailored for PHP development but also supports web technologies like HTML, CSS, and JavaScript. It offers excellent PHP support, intelligent coding assistance, and seamless integration with databases.

3. Choosing the Right Tool

When selecting a code editor or IDE, consider the following factors:

- **Language Support:** Ensure that the tool supports the programming languages and frameworks you plan to use.

- **Extensions and Plugins:** Check the availability of extensions or plugins that enhance your workflow.

- **Performance:** Evaluate the tool's speed and responsiveness, especially when working on large projects.

- **Ease of Use**: Choose a tool that matches your preferences in terms of user interface and customization.

- **Community and Support:** Look for an active community and ample online resources for troubleshooting and learning.

- **Cost:** Consider your budget, as some IDEs may require a paid license.

Ultimately, the choice between a code editor and an IDE depends on your workflow, preferences, and project requirements. Experiment with different tools to find the one that best suits your needs and enhances your productivity as a web developer.

6.2 Browser Developer Tools

Browser Developer Tools are a set of built-in utilities provided by web browsers to help developers inspect, debug, and optimize web pages and applications. These tools are invaluable for web developers and designers to understand how their code is executed and to diagnose and fix issues. In this section, we'll explore the capabilities and usage of browser developer tools.

1. Accessing Developer Tools

To access browser developer tools, follow these common keyboard shortcuts or menu options:

- **Google Chrome:** Press `Ctrl+Shift+I` (Windows/Linux) or `Cmd+Option+I` (Mac), or right-click on a page element and select "Inspect."

- **Mozilla Firefox:** Press `Ctrl+Shift+I` (Windows/Linux) or `Cmd+Option+I` (Mac), or right-click on a page element and select "Inspect Element."

- **Microsoft Edge:** Press `Ctrl+Shift+I` (Windows/Linux) or `Cmd+Option+I` (Mac), or right-click on a page element and select "Inspect Element."

2. Elements Panel

The Elements panel allows you to inspect and modify the HTML and CSS of a web page in real-time. Here's what you can do with it:

- **Inspect Elements:** Click on elements in the panel to highlight corresponding parts of the page on the screen.

- **Edit HTML and CSS:** Double-click on HTML elements or CSS styles to edit them directly in the panel, seeing the changes reflected immediately.

- **Navigate the DOM:** View the page's Document Object Model (DOM) tree, showing the hierarchical structure of elements.

3. Console Panel

The Console panel is where you can interact with the JavaScript code running on the page. You can use it for:

- **Debugging:** Log messages, errors, and warnings generated by your JavaScript code using `console.log()`, `console.error()`, and other console methods.

- **Executing Code:** Enter and run JavaScript code snippets directly in the console to experiment or diagnose issues.

- **Profiling Performance:** Analyze and profile your code's performance using built-in profiling tools.

4. Sources Panel

The Sources panel is your JavaScript debugging hub. You can:

- **Set Breakpoints:** Add breakpoints to your JavaScript code to pause execution and inspect variables at specific points.

- **Step Through Code:** Execute code step by step, including stepping into functions and out of them.

- **Watch Expressions:** Monitor the values of specific variables or expressions during debugging.

5. Network Panel

The Network panel tracks all network requests made by the web page, including:

- **HTTP Requests:** View details of requests and responses, such as headers, status codes, and timings.

- **Resource Loading:** Identify slow or failed requests, optimize resource loading, and diagnose connectivity issues.

6. Performance Panel

The Performance panel helps you analyze and improve the page's overall performance by recording and analyzing its activities, including:

- **Recording:** Start and stop performance recordings to capture interactions and resource loading.

- **Analyzing:** Visualize and analyze performance bottlenecks and issues with the timeline view.

- **Auditing:** Generate performance reports and recommendations to improve page speed and responsiveness.

7. Application Panel

The Application panel provides insights into web application behavior, including:

- **Storage:** Manage and inspect cookies, local storage, session storage, and indexedDB data.

- **Service Workers:** Debug and manage service workers for Progressive Web Apps (PWAs).

8. Security Panel

The Security panel helps you identify and resolve security issues by providing information about the page's security features and potential threats, including:

- **HTTPS:** Check for secure (HTTPS) connections and mixed content issues.

- **Security Headers:** Analyze the presence and configuration of security headers.

Browser developer tools are a fundamental part of the web development process. They empower developers to create better, faster, and more secure web applications by allowing them to inspect, debug, and optimize code in real-time. As you become proficient with these tools, you'll find yourself more capable of building high-quality web experiences.

6.3 Version Control with Git and GitHub

Version control is a critical tool in the world of web development, allowing developers to track changes to their code, collaborate with others, and manage complex projects efficiently. Git is a distributed version control system, and GitHub is a popular platform for hosting Git repositories. In this section, we'll explore the fundamentals of version control with Git and how to use GitHub for collaboration.

1. Introduction to Version Control

Version control is the practice of tracking and managing changes to your code over time. It provides several key benefits:

- **History Tracking:** You can view a complete history of changes, who made them, and when they were made.

- **Collaboration:** Multiple developers can work on the same project simultaneously without conflicts.

- **Backup and Recovery:** Your code is safely stored on remote servers, reducing the risk of data loss.

2. Getting Started with Git

To start using Git, follow these basic steps:

- Installation: Download and install Git on your computer.

- Configuration: Set up your name and email address in Git's configuration.

- Initialization: Create a new Git repository for your project using `git init`.

3. Basic Git Commands

Here are some essential Git commands you should know:

- `git status`: Check the status of your repository, including changes to be committed.

- `git add`: Stage changes for commit.

- `git commit`: Create a new commit with staged changes and a descriptive message.

- `git log`: View the commit history.

- `git branch`: List, create, or delete branches.

- `git checkout`: Switch between branches.

4. Collaborating with Git

When working with others, you'll need to interact with remote repositories. GitHub is a popular platform for hosting remote Git repositories. Key actions include:

- **Cloning a Repository**: Use `git clone` to copy a remote repository to your local machine.

- **Pulling Changes:** `git pull` fetches changes from the remote repository and merges them into your local branch.

- **Pushing Changes:** `git push` uploads your local commits to the remote repository.

- **Forking and Pull Requests:** Fork a repository on GitHub to create your own copy. You can then submit pull requests to contribute changes back to the original repository.

5. Branching and Merging

Git allows you to create branches to work on new features or bug fixes independently. You can then merge these branches back into the main codebase. Key concepts include:

- **Feature Branches:** Create a new branch for each new feature or bug fix.

- **Merging:** Use `git merge` to combine changes from one branch into another.

- **Conflict Resolution:** Handle merge conflicts when Git can't automatically merge changes.

6. Best Practices

To use Git effectively, consider these best practices:

- **Commit Often:** Make small, focused commits with descriptive messages.

- **Use Branches:** Create feature branches to isolate changes and merge them when they're ready.

- **Write Meaningful Commit Messages:** Describe the purpose of your commits clearly.

- **Pull Frequently:** Keep your local repository up to date by pulling changes from the remote regularly.

- **Collaborate Effectively:** Communicate with your team and follow branching and pull request workflows.

Version control with Git and platforms like GitHub is crucial for web development projects of any size. It enables efficient collaboration, maintains a complete history of changes, and provides a safety net for code recovery. Whether you're working on a personal project or contributing to open-source software, mastering Git and GitHub will significantly improve your development workflow.

6.4 Web Development Extensions and Plugins

In the world of web development, extensions and plugins are valuable tools that can enhance your productivity and efficiency. These browser add-ons and integrated development environment (IDE) extensions provide various functionalities, from debugging to code optimization. In this section, we'll explore some of the most useful web development extensions and plugins that can make your development workflow smoother.

1. Browser Developer Tools

Modern web browsers come equipped with built-in developer tools that are indispensable for web development. Here's how you can use them:

- **Inspect Element:** Right-click on any element on a web page and select "Inspect" to examine its HTML and CSS.

- **Console:** The console allows you to run JavaScript code and view error messages. It's essential for debugging.

- **Network Tab:** Monitor network requests to optimize load times and check for errors.

- **Sources Tab:** Debug JavaScript using breakpoints and step-by-step execution.

- **Audits Tab:** Analyze web page performance and get suggestions for improvements.

2. Code Editors and IDE Extensions

Many code editors and integrated development environments offer extensions and plugins to enhance your coding experience. Here are some popular ones:

- **Visual Studio Code (VS Code)**: VS Code has a vast marketplace of extensions. Some popular ones include "Live Server" for live preview and "Prettier" for code formatting.

- **Sublime Text**: Sublime Text supports packages like "Emmet" for HTML/CSS abbreviation and "Git" for version control integration.

- **Atom:** Atom offers extensions like "Minimap" for code navigation and "Linter" for real-time code linting.

3. Browser Extensions

Browser extensions can be incredibly helpful for various web development tasks:

- **Web Developer:** This extension provides a wide range of web development tools, including options for disabling JavaScript and CSS, resizing the browser window, and viewing responsive layouts.

- **ColorZilla**: ColorZilla allows you to pick colors from web pages and generate CSS color codes.

- **JSON Formatter:** If you work with JSON data, this extension formats and highlights JSON for easier reading.

- **SEOquake:** SEOquake provides SEO-related information about a webpage, including Google PageRank and keyword density.

4. IDE-Specific Extensions

If you use a specific IDE for web development, there are often extensions tailored to your needs:

- **Eclipse:** Eclipse offers extensions for web development, including plugins for HTML, CSS, and JavaScript support.

- **NetBeans**: NetBeans has plugins like "JavaScript Editor" and "HTML5/JavaScript" that provide enhanced support for web development.

- **IntelliJ IDEA:** IntelliJ IDEA offers extensions like "WebStorm" that cater to web developers, with features like HTML and JavaScript support.

5. Accessibility Tools

Web accessibility is crucial, and there are extensions to help you ensure your web projects are accessible to all users:

- **axe:** The axe extension helps you identify and fix accessibility issues in your web applications.

- **WAVE Evaluation Tool**: WAVE evaluates web content for accessibility issues directly in your browser.

These are just a few examples of the many web development extensions and plugins available. Depending on your specific needs and the tools you use, you can customize your development environment to be more efficient and effective. Explore these extensions, and don't hesitate to try out new ones to find the ones that work best for your workflow.

CHAPTER VII
Putting It All Together: Practical Projects

7.1 Project 1: Personal Portfolio Website

In this chapter, we'll embark on a practical journey by creating your very own personal portfolio website. A portfolio website is an essential asset for any aspiring web developer or designer to showcase their skills, projects, and achievements. By the end of this project, you'll have a stunning online portfolio that you can share with potential employers and clients.

Project Overview:

Your personal portfolio website will consist of the following key components:

1. Home Page: This is the first page visitors will see. It should introduce you, provide a brief overview of your skills and interests, and encourage users to explore further.

2. About Page: The about page offers a more detailed look at your background, experience, and personal story. You can include your education, work history, and any relevant personal details.

3. Portfolio Page: Showcase your best work in this section. Include descriptions, images, and links to your projects. Make it visually appealing and easy to navigate.

4. Contact Page: Allow visitors to get in touch with you. You can include a contact form, your email address, and links to your social media profiles.

Project Steps:

Here's a step-by-step guide on how to create your personal portfolio website:

Step 1: Planning

- Define your website's purpose and target audience.

- Sketch out a rough layout for your website's pages.

- Decide on a color scheme and design aesthetic that represents you.

Step 2: Setting Up Your Development Environment

- Choose a code editor or IDE that you're comfortable with.

- Create a new project folder for your website.

Step 3: Building the Structure

- Start with the HTML structure of your pages. Create the necessary HTML files for each page (e.g., index.html, about.html, portfolio.html, contact.html).

- Use semantic HTML elements to structure your content.

Step 4: Adding Style with CSS

- Create a CSS file (e.g., styles.css) to style your website.

- Apply CSS rules to control the layout, typography, colors, and overall design of your pages.

Step 5: Making it Responsive

- Ensure your website looks and functions well on various devices and screen sizes using media queries.

- Implement responsive design principles to adapt your layout.

Step 6: Adding Interactivity with JavaScript (Optional)

- Enhance user experience by adding interactive features such as smooth scrolling, navigation menus, or animations using JavaScript.

Step 7: Populating Content

- Write compelling and concise content for each page. Focus on clarity and relevance.

- Create a portfolio section where you can showcase your projects. Include images, project descriptions, and links to the live projects or code repositories.

Step 8: Contact Form (Optional)

- If you choose to include a contact form, set up the necessary back-end functionality to handle form submissions.

- Validate user input to prevent spam and ensure data integrity.

Step 9: Testing and Debugging

- Thoroughly test your website on different browsers and devices to catch and fix any compatibility issues.

- Debug any errors or issues in your code.

Step 10: Deployment

- Choose a hosting platform for your website. Options include GitHub Pages, Netlify, or traditional web hosting providers.

- Configure domain settings if you have a custom domain.

Step 11: Launch and Share

- Once your website is live, share it with your network, including friends, family, and potential employers or clients.

- Promote your portfolio on social media and professional networking sites.

By the end of this project, you'll not only have a fully functional and visually appealing portfolio website but also valuable experience in web development and design. This project will serve as a showcase of your skills and a platform to kickstart your web development career or freelance journey. Enjoy the process of creating your personal portfolio website!

7.2 Project 2: Interactive Photo Gallery

In this practical project, you'll learn how to create an interactive photo gallery for your website. Photo galleries are a popular feature for showcasing images in an engaging and visually appealing way. By the end of this project, you'll have a functional photo gallery that allows users to view and interact with your images.

Project Overview:

Your interactive photo gallery will include the following key features:

1. Thumbnail Display: Display a grid of thumbnail images that represent the photos in your gallery.

2. Image Viewer: When a user clicks on a thumbnail, it should open a larger view of the image in a lightbox or modal window.

3. Navigation: Allow users to navigate between images in the viewer, either through buttons or keyboard shortcuts.

4. Image Descriptions: Include optional captions or descriptions for each image.

Project Steps:

Here's a step-by-step guide on how to create your interactive photo gallery:

Step 1: Planning

- Determine the purpose and content of your photo gallery.

- Decide how many images you want to include and gather them in a folder.

Step 2: Setting Up Your Development Environment

- Choose a code editor or IDE.

- Create a new project folder for your photo gallery.

Step 3: HTML Structure

- Create an HTML file (e.g., gallery.html) to structure your photo gallery.

- Define the HTML structure for thumbnails, the image viewer, and any additional elements.

Step 4: CSS Styling

- Create a CSS file (e.g., styles.css) to style your photo gallery.

- Style the thumbnail grid, image viewer, and any navigation elements.

Step 5: JavaScript Functionality

- Write JavaScript code to handle interactions:

  - Load the list of images.

  - Generate thumbnails dynamically.

  - Implement the lightbox/modal functionality.

  - Enable image navigation.

Step 6: Image Descriptions (Optional)

- If you want to include image descriptions, add them in your HTML and style them with CSS.

- Use JavaScript to display descriptions when an image is viewed.

Step 7: Testing and Debugging

- Test your photo gallery on various browsers and devices to ensure compatibility.

- Debug any JavaScript or CSS issues that may arise.

Step 8: Deployment

- Choose a hosting platform for your website.

- Upload your photo gallery project to your chosen hosting provider.

Step 9: Launch and Share

- Share your interactive photo gallery with others, whether it's friends, family, or website visitors.

- Promote your gallery on your portfolio website or social media.

By completing this project, you'll not only have a functional interactive photo gallery but also valuable experience in front-end web development, including HTML, CSS, and JavaScript. This project can enhance the visual appeal of your portfolio and demonstrate your skills in creating user-friendly and interactive web features. Enjoy building your photo gallery!

7.3 Project 3: Contact Form with Server-Side Integration

In this practical project, you'll learn how to create a contact form for your website and integrate it with server-side technology to handle form submissions. Contact forms are a crucial component of websites, enabling visitors to get in touch with you or your organization. By the end of this project, you'll have a functional contact form that can collect user input and send it to your email or a server for processing.

Project Overview:

Your contact form project will include the following key features:

1. Form Fields: Create input fields for common contact form elements, such as name, email, subject, and message.

2. Validation: Implement client-side validation to ensure that users enter valid information before submission.

3. Server-Side Integration: Set up a server or use existing server-side technology (e.g., PHP, Node.js) to process form submissions.

4. Email Notifications: Configure your server to send email notifications when a user submits the form.

5. Confirmation Page: Redirect users to a confirmation page after successful submission.

Project Steps:

Here's a step-by-step guide on how to create your contact form with server-side integration:

Step 1: Planning

- Determine the specific fields you want to include in your contact form.

- Decide whether you want to build a server-side script or use a service like Formspree or Netlify Forms to handle form submissions.

Step 2: Setting Up Your Development Environment

- Choose a code editor or IDE.

- Create a new project folder for your contact form.

Step 3: HTML Form Structure

- Create an HTML file (e.g., contact.html) to structure your contact form.

- Define the HTML form elements, including input fields, labels, and a submit button.

Step 4: Client-Side Validation

- Write JavaScript code to validate user input on the client side.

- Ensure that required fields are filled out correctly before submission.

Step 5: Server-Side Integration

- Depending on your chosen server-side technology, create a server file (e.g., server.js for Node.js or contact.php for PHP).

- Configure your server to handle POST requests from the form.

Step 6: Email Configuration

- Set up email sending functionality within your server code.

- Use a library or module (e.g., Nodemailer for Node.js) to send email notifications to your desired recipient.

Step 7: Confirmation Page

- Create a confirmation page (e.g., confirmation.html) to display a thank-you message after successful submission.

- Redirect users to this page upon successful form submission.

Step 8: Testing

- Test your contact form thoroughly, both for client-side validation and server-side functionality.

- Ensure that email notifications are sent as expected.

Step 9: Deployment

- Choose a hosting platform for your website.

- Upload your contact form project and server-side code to your chosen hosting provider.

Step 10: Launch and Share

- Make your contact form live on your website, allowing visitors to reach out to you.

- Promote the availability of your contact form through your website's navigation or a dedicated "Contact" page.

By completing this project, you'll not only have a functional contact form on your website but also a valuable understanding of handling form submissions on the server side. A contact form is an essential tool for communication with your website's audience, clients, or potential employers. Enjoy building and integrating your contact form with server-side technology!

CHAPTER VIII
Web Hosting and Deployment

8.1 Choosing a Domain Name

Selecting the right domain name is a critical step in establishing your online presence. Your domain name serves as your website's unique address on the internet, making it essential to choose a name that is memorable, relevant, and represents your brand or website effectively. In this section, we will explore the process of choosing a domain name that aligns with your goals and resonates with your target audience.

Key Considerations:

1. Relevance to Your Content: Your domain name should reflect the purpose or content of your website. It should give visitors a clear idea of what to expect when they visit your site. For example, if your website is about travel photography, a domain name like "TravelSnapshots.com" would be relevant.

2. Memorability: A good domain name is easy to remember. Avoid complex or lengthy names that may confuse visitors. Short, catchy, and memorable names tend to work best.

3. Avoid Special Characters and Hyphens: Stick to alphanumeric characters and avoid special characters or hyphens. Simple, uncluttered domain names are more user-friendly.

4. Branding: If you're creating a website for your business or personal brand, consider using your brand name as the domain. Consistency in branding is essential.

5. Keyword Research: If your website's primary purpose is to attract organic traffic, conduct keyword research to identify relevant keywords that can be included in your domain name. Keywords can improve your website's search engine visibility.

6. Domain Extensions: Decide on the domain extension (also known as a top-level domain or TLD). Common extensions include .com, .org, .net, and many more. Choose an extension that aligns with your website's purpose. While .com is the most popular, other extensions may be more suitable for specific niches (e.g., .io for tech startups).

Steps to Choose a Domain Name:

1. Brainstorm Ideas: Start by brainstorming domain name ideas that reflect your website's content or purpose. Write down as many options as possible.

2. Check Availability: Use a domain registrar or domain search tool to check the availability of your desired domain names. It's possible that your first choice may already be registered. Be prepared with alternatives.

3. Avoid Copyright Issues: Ensure that your chosen domain name does not infringe on trademarks or copyrights. Check the databases of trademark offices or consult with a legal expert if needed.

4. Consider Future Growth: Think about your long-term goals. Will your website's content expand beyond its current focus? Choose a domain name that accommodates potential growth.

5. Keep It Simple: Simplicity is key. Avoid complex spellings, slang, or obscure references that could confuse your audience.

6. Purchase and Register: Once you've selected your domain name, proceed to purchase and register it through a domain registrar. Most registrars offer additional services like domain privacy protection and email hosting.

7. Renew Your Domain: Keep track of your domain's expiration date and renew it promptly to prevent losing ownership.

Examples:

Let's consider a few examples of domain names and the principles behind them:

1. Website Type: Travel Blog

   - **Domain Name:** AdventureExplorer.com

   - **Explanation:** The domain name clearly indicates that the website is about travel adventures and exploration.

2. Website Type: Personal Portfolio

   - **Domain Name:** JohnSmithDesigns.com

   - **Explanation:** Using the individual's name and "designs" indicates that this is a portfolio website for John Smith's design work.

3. Website Type: Tech Startup

   - **Domain Name:** TechWizards.io

   - **Explanation:** The .io extension is commonly used by tech startups, and the name implies expertise in technology.

Choosing the right domain name may take some time and research, but it's a critical step in establishing your online presence. A well-chosen domain name can make your website more accessible and memorable to your audience.

8.2 Selecting a Web Hosting Provider

Choosing the right web hosting provider is a crucial decision when bringing your website online. A reliable hosting provider ensures that your website is accessible to visitors, offers sufficient resources, and provides support when needed. In this section, we'll explore the steps and considerations for selecting a web hosting provider that suits your needs.

Key Considerations:

1. Hosting Type: Determine the type of hosting that aligns with your website's requirements. Common hosting types include shared hosting, VPS (Virtual Private Server) hosting, dedicated hosting, and cloud hosting. Each has its own advantages and limitations.

2. Server Location: Consider the geographical location of the hosting provider's servers. Select a location that is closest to your target audience to minimize latency and improve website performance.

3. Uptime and Reliability: Check the hosting provider's uptime guarantees and reliability records. Aim for a provider with at least a 99.9% uptime guarantee.

4. Scalability: Assess whether the hosting provider allows for easy scaling as your website grows. You should be able to upgrade or downgrade your hosting plan as needed.

5. Resource Allocation: Understand the resources allocated with your hosting plan, including storage, bandwidth, CPU, RAM, and database capacity. Ensure that they meet your website's requirements.

6. Security Features: Look for hosting providers that offer security features such as SSL certificates, firewalls, DDoS protection, and regular backups. Website security is critical.

7. Customer Support: Evaluate the level of customer support provided. 24/7 customer support with multiple contact channels (e.g., live chat, email, phone) can be beneficial.

8. User-Friendly Control Panel: A user-friendly control panel, such as cPanel or Plesk, makes it easier to manage your hosting account, domains, and website files.

9. Add-Ons and Features: Check if the hosting provider offers additional features, like one-click app installations (e.g., WordPress), email hosting, and domain registration services.

10. Cost: Compare hosting plans and pricing. Be aware of any hidden fees or renewal price increases. Consider your budget and long-term hosting costs.

Steps to Select a Web Hosting Provider:

1. Research and List Options: Start by researching different hosting providers and creating a list of potential candidates. Read reviews, seek recommendations, and consider your specific hosting needs.

2. Assess Hosting Types: Determine the type of hosting you need based on your website's size and complexity. Shared hosting is suitable for small websites, while larger sites may require VPS or dedicated hosting.

3. Check Uptime and Reliability: Research the uptime records and reliability history of the hosting providers on your list. Look for customer feedback and reviews regarding downtime.

4. Review Resource Allocation: Ensure that the hosting plans you're considering provide adequate resources for your website. Avoid plans with strict resource limitations.

5. Evaluate Security Measures: Security is paramount. Confirm that the hosting provider offers essential security features and practices. Consider if they provide SSL certificates for secure connections.

6. Test Customer Support: Reach out to the hosting providers' support teams with questions or concerns to gauge their responsiveness and helpfulness.

7. Explore Control Panels: If possible, explore the control panels offered by each hosting provider. A demo or trial can help you assess their user-friendliness.

8. Consider Add-Ons: Take into account any additional services or features offered by the hosting provider, such as website builders, domain registration, or marketing tools.

9. Compare Pricing: Compare the pricing of hosting plans, considering both the initial cost and renewal rates. Pay attention to the features included in each plan.

10. Read Terms and Conditions: Review the terms of service and hosting agreements to understand the provider's policies on issues like data usage, refunds, and resource allocation.

Example Hosting Providers:

1. Bluehost: Known for its WordPress-friendly hosting and strong customer support.

2. SiteGround: Offers excellent performance and security features, especially for WordPress websites.

3. HostGator: Provides a range of hosting options and a user-friendly control panel.

4. A2 Hosting: Known for its speed and developer-friendly features.

5. InMotion Hosting: Offers a variety of hosting types and has a reputation for reliability.

Remember that the hosting provider you choose can significantly impact your website's performance and reliability. Take the time to research and select a provider that aligns with your specific needs and goals.

8.3 Uploading Your Website

Once you've chosen a domain name, selected a web hosting provider, and built your website, the next step is to upload your website to the hosting server. This process involves transferring your website's files, databases, and other assets to the web server where they will be publicly accessible. Here's a detailed guide on how to upload your website:

1. Prepare Your Website Files:

Before uploading, make sure your website files are well-organized. Your website's main files may include HTML, CSS, JavaScript, images, and other assets. Ensure all file paths in your code are correct.

2. Choose a File Transfer Method:

There are several methods for uploading files to a web server:

- **File Transfer Protocol (FTP):** FTP is a standard method for transferring files to a server. You'll need an FTP client like FileZilla or Cyberduck. Enter your server's FTP credentials (provided by your hosting provider) and connect to the server.

- **File Manager in cPanel:** Many hosting providers offer cPanel, a web-based control panel. You can use the File Manager in cPanel to upload files directly from your web browser.

- **SSH/SFTP:** If you're comfortable with the command line, you can use SSH (Secure Shell) and SFTP (SSH File Transfer Protocol) for secure file uploads.

3. Connect to Your Server:

Regardless of the method you choose, you'll need to connect to your web server using the provided server credentials. This typically includes the server address, username, and password.

4. Navigate to the Website Root Directory:

Access the root directory of your website on the server. This is usually a folder named "public_html," "www," or something similar. Files placed here will be publicly accessible on the internet.

5. Upload Your Files:

Using your chosen method, navigate to your local website folder and select all the files you want to upload. Then, drag and drop or use the "Upload" button to transfer them to the server.

6. Set File Permissions:

Make sure your files and directories have the correct permissions. Generally, directories should have permissions of 755, and files should have permissions of 644. Your FTP client or file manager usually provides an option to change permissions.

7. Test Your Website:

After uploading your files, test your website to ensure that it works as expected on the live server. Check for broken links, missing assets, and any issues that might have arisen during the upload process.

8. Configure Databases (If Applicable):

If your website relies on a database, you'll need to create a database on the server, import your local database, and update your website's configuration files with the new database credentials.

9. Update DNS Records:

If you're changing web hosting providers or domain registrars, you might need to update your domain's DNS (Domain Name System) records to point to the new server. This step can take some time to propagate across the internet.

10. Backup Your Website:

Always keep backups of your website files and databases. Regular backups are essential for disaster recovery and version control.

11. Monitor and Troubleshoot:

After the upload, monitor your website for any issues. Be prepared to troubleshoot and fix any problems that may arise, such as broken links, missing files, or server-related issues.

12. Update Your Website:

As your website evolves, continue to upload new or updated files to keep it current. Use the same file transfer methods and ensure that changes are reflected accurately on the live site.

Remember that the process of uploading your website can vary depending on your hosting provider and the tools available. Always refer to your hosting provider's documentation or support for specific instructions tailored to your hosting environment.

8.4 Testing and Troubleshooting

Testing and troubleshooting are crucial steps in the web hosting and deployment process. Ensuring that your website works correctly and identifying and resolving any issues are essential before launching your site to the public. Here's a detailed guide on how to test and troubleshoot your website:

1. Pre-Launch Testing:

Before making your website live, conduct thorough testing to catch and fix any issues. This includes:

- **Cross-Browser Testing:** Test your website on various web browsers (e.g., Chrome, Firefox, Safari, Edge) to ensure compatibility. Pay attention to how your site renders and functions on each browser.

- **Responsiveness:** Check how your site appears on different devices (desktops, tablets, smartphones) to ensure it's responsive and mobile-friendly.

- **Navigation:** Test all navigation elements, links, and buttons to ensure they work correctly. Make sure users can easily navigate through your site.

- **Forms:** If your site includes forms, test them thoroughly to ensure they submit data as expected. Check for validation, error handling, and confirmation messages.

- **Performance:** Use tools like Google PageSpeed Insights or GTmetrix to evaluate your site's loading speed. Optimize images and scripts for faster load times.

- **SEO:** Verify that your site's pages have proper meta tags, titles, and descriptions for search engine optimization (SEO). Use SEO auditing tools to identify issues.

- **Content Check:** Proofread and review all content for accuracy, grammar, and spelling errors. Ensure images and multimedia display correctly.

2. Functional Testing:

Perform functional testing to ensure all features and functionality of your website work as intended. This includes:

- **User Registration and Login:** Test user registration and login processes if applicable. Check for account creation, password reset, and user authentication.

- **E-commerce Features:** If your site has e-commerce functionality, test product listings, shopping carts, and the checkout process. Verify payment gateway integration.

- **Database Functionality:** Test any database-driven features such as dynamic content, search functionality, and user-generated content.

- **Interactive Elements:** Check interactive elements like sliders, carousels, accordions, and pop-up modals for proper behavior.

3. Compatibility and Performance Testing:

- Check Different Devices: Ensure your website performs well on various devices, including smartphones, tablets, and desktop computers.

- Cross-Platform Testing: Test your site on different operating systems (Windows, macOS, Linux) to check for any platform-specific issues.

4. Security Testing:

Security is paramount for a live website. Test for vulnerabilities such as SQL injection, cross-site scripting (XSS), and cross-site request forgery (CSRF). Use security scanning tools or consult a security expert.

5. Load Testing:

Simulate heavy traffic to your website to assess its performance under load. Tools like Apache JMeter or LoadRunner can help you identify potential bottlenecks.

6. Accessibility Testing:

Ensure that your website is accessible to individuals with disabilities. Test for compliance with Web Content Accessibility Guidelines (WCAG) using accessibility testing tools.

7. Troubleshooting:

Identify and address any issues or errors you encounter during testing. Log and document any problems you find and systematically resolve them. Common troubleshooting steps include:

- Checking server logs for errors.

- Debugging code to find and fix issues.

- Validating and correcting broken links.

- Addressing layout and design problems.

- Investigating slow loading times and optimizing.

- Resolving database connection issues.

8. Continuous Monitoring:

After launching your website, continue monitoring it for performance, security, and functionality issues. Implement website monitoring tools and establish a process for regular updates and maintenance.

9. User Testing:

Consider conducting user testing with a group of real users to gather feedback on usability and user experience. Use their input to make improvements.

10. Backup and Rollback Plan:

Always have a backup of your website before making any significant changes. If issues arise after deployment, you can roll back to a working version.

By thoroughly testing and troubleshooting your website, you can ensure a smoother and more reliable experience for your users and mitigate issues that may negatively impact your online presence.

8.5 Launching Your Website

Launching your website is an exciting moment, but it requires careful planning and execution to ensure a smooth and successful transition from development to the live environment. Here's a detailed guide on how to launch your website:

1. Final Testing:

Before launching your website, conduct a final round of testing to ensure that everything is working correctly. This includes:

- **Cross-Browser Testing:** Verify that your site functions well on different web browsers.

- **Responsiveness:** Ensure that your site is fully responsive on various devices, including smartphones and tablets.

- **Links and Navigation:** Double-check all links and navigation elements to make sure they work as intended.

- **Forms:** Test any forms on your site to confirm that data submission and validation work correctly.

- **Performance:** Optimize your site's performance by addressing any last-minute speed issues.

2. Backup Your Website:

Before making any changes to your live site, create a full backup of your website. This ensures that you can quickly restore your site if anything goes wrong during the launch process.

3. Domain and Hosting Setup:

Ensure that your domain name is correctly configured to point to your web hosting server. Check that your hosting environment is ready to receive your website files.

4. Upload Your Website:

Upload all your website files to the appropriate directories on your web hosting server. Use a secure file transfer method such as SFTP or SSH to protect your data during transmission.

5. Configure DNS Settings:

If your domain is registered with a different provider than your hosting, you'll need to configure DNS settings to point your domain to your hosting server. This may involve setting up A records or name servers.

6. Database Setup (If Applicable):

If your website relies on a database, make sure it's set up correctly on your hosting server, and update your website's configuration files with the new database connection details.

7. SSL Certificate Installation:

Consider installing an SSL certificate to secure your website with HTTPS. Many hosting providers offer free SSL certificates through Let's Encrypt.

8. Test the Live Site:

Once your website is live, thoroughly test it to ensure that everything functions correctly in the live environment. Pay attention to the following:

- Links and navigation.

- Forms and user interactions.

- Performance and loading times.

- Database-driven content (if applicable).

- SSL encryption and security.

9. Monitor Website Traffic:

After the launch, monitor your website's traffic and performance using web analytics tools like Google Analytics. Check for any sudden issues that may arise.

10. Announce the Launch:

Let your audience know that your website is live. Announce it through your social media channels, email newsletters, and any other relevant communication methods.

11. SEO and Sitemap Submission:

Update your sitemap and submit it to search engines like Google and Bing. Ensure that your meta tags, titles, and descriptions are optimized for SEO.

12. Backup After Launch:

Take another backup of your website now that it's live. Regularly back up your site to ensure you have a recent copy in case of any issues.

13. Continuous Maintenance:

Websites require ongoing maintenance. Regularly update content, check for broken links, and apply security patches and updates to your site's CMS and plugins.

14. Monitor and Troubleshoot:

Continuously monitor your website's performance, security, and user feedback. Be prepared to troubleshoot and resolve any issues that may arise.

Launching your website is a significant milestone, but it's just the beginning of your online journey. By following these steps, you can ensure a successful launch and maintain a high-quality website for your visitors.

CHAPTER IX
Web Development Best Practices

9.1 Writing Clean and Maintainable Code

Writing clean and maintainable code is essential for the long-term success and sustainability of any web development project. Clean code is easier to understand, modify, and extend, reducing the likelihood of introducing bugs and making collaboration with other developers more efficient. In this section, we will explore best practices for writing clean and maintainable code.

1. Use Meaningful Variable and Function Names:

Choose descriptive and self-explanatory names for variables and functions. Avoid vague names like "x" or "temp" and opt for names that reflect the purpose and content of the variable or function.

```javascript
// Bad variable name
let x = 10;


// Good variable name
let numberOfItems = 10;
```

```
```

2. Follow Coding Conventions:

Adhere to a consistent coding style and follow established coding conventions for your chosen programming language. This includes indentation, naming conventions, and the use of brackets.

3. Keep Functions Small:

Write functions that do one thing and do it well. Functions should have a single responsibility and be concise. If a function becomes too long or complex, consider breaking it into smaller, reusable functions.

4. Comment Your Code:

Use comments to explain complex logic, algorithmic choices, and any non-obvious code. However, strive to write code that is self-documenting by using meaningful names and clear structure.

5. Avoid Magic Numbers and Strings:

Avoid hardcoding values directly into your code, as they can be difficult to maintain and change later. Instead, use constants or variables with meaningful names.

```javascript
// Magic number
if (age >= 18) {
```

```
  // Do something
}


// Better
const legalAge = 18;
if (age >= legalAge) {
  // Do something
}
```

6. Modularize Your Code:

Break your code into reusable modules or components. This promotes code reusability, readability, and makes it easier to maintain and test individual parts of your application.

7. Error Handling:

Implement proper error handling by using try-catch blocks or error-handling middleware. Handle errors gracefully and provide meaningful error messages to aid in debugging.

8. Testing and Test-Driven Development (TDD):

Write unit tests for your code to ensure it functions correctly. Consider adopting Test-Driven Development (TDD) practices where you write tests before writing the actual code.

9. Version Control:

Use version control systems like Git to track changes, collaborate with others, and easily revert to previous versions if issues arise.

10. Refactor Regularly:

Refactoring is the process of improving the structure and readability of your code without changing its behavior. Regularly review your code and refactor as needed to keep it clean and maintainable.

11. Code Reviews:

Encourage code reviews within your development team. Peer reviews help identify issues, share knowledge, and maintain code quality.

12. Documentation:

Document your code, APIs, and usage instructions. Clear documentation makes it easier for other developers (including future you) to understand and work with your code.

13. Stay Updated:

Keep up with best practices, coding standards, and changes in the web development ecosystem. Technology evolves rapidly, and staying informed is crucial for writing modern, maintainable code.

By following these best practices, you can write code that is not only functional but also clean, maintainable, and conducive to collaborative development. Clean code reduces technical debt and contributes to the long-term success of your web development projects.

9.2 Performance Optimization

Performance optimization is a critical aspect of web development. A fast and responsive website not only provides a better user experience but also positively impacts search engine rankings and user engagement. In this section, we will explore various techniques and best practices to optimize the performance of your web applications.

1. Minimize HTTP Requests:

Reducing the number of HTTP requests is one of the most effective ways to improve website performance. Combine CSS and JavaScript files, use image sprites, and minimize the use of external resources.

2. Use Content Delivery Networks (CDNs):

Leverage CDNs to serve static assets like images, stylesheets, and scripts from servers located closer to your users. This reduces latency and speeds up content delivery.

3. Optimize Images:

Compress and resize images to reduce their file size while maintaining acceptable quality. Use modern image formats like WebP, and consider lazy loading images to improve page load times.

4. Enable Browser Caching:

Leverage browser caching by setting appropriate cache headers for your static assets. This allows the browser to store resources locally, reducing the need to download them on subsequent visits.

5. Minify and Bundle CSS and JavaScript:

Minify your CSS and JavaScript files to remove unnecessary whitespace and comments. Bundle multiple files into a single file to reduce the number of requests.

6. Optimize Critical Rendering Path:

Ensure that the critical resources needed to render the visible portion of a web page (e.g., HTML, CSS, and JavaScript) are delivered quickly to improve the initial page load time.

7. Use Asynchronous Loading:

Load non-essential scripts and assets asynchronously to prevent them from blocking the rendering of the page. Consider using the "async" and "defer" attributes for scripts.

8. Compress Content:

Enable gzip or Brotli compression on your web server to reduce the size of text-based assets, such as HTML, CSS, and JavaScript files.

9. Minimize Redirects:

Minimize the use of URL redirects, as each redirect adds an additional HTTP request and increases page load time.

10. Prioritize Above-the-Fold Content:

Optimize the content that appears above the fold (visible part of the webpage without scrolling) to load quickly. Lazy-load below-the-fold content.

11. Reduce Server Response Time:

Optimize your server-side code, database queries, and server configurations to reduce server response times. Consider using caching mechanisms.

12. Monitor and Analyze Performance:

Use web performance monitoring tools like Google PageSpeed Insights, GTmetrix, or WebPageTest to identify bottlenecks and areas for improvement.

13. Mobile Optimization:

Ensure that your website is responsive and optimized for mobile devices. Consider using responsive design techniques and implementing Accelerated Mobile Pages (AMP).

14. Remove Unused Code and Dependencies:

Regularly review and remove unused code, libraries, and dependencies from your project to reduce its overall size.

15. Content Delivery Strategies:

Implement lazy loading for images and implement strategies like code-splitting to load only the necessary code for a specific page or feature.

16. Use Web Workers:

Leverage web workers to offload CPU-intensive tasks to separate threads, improving the responsiveness of your web application.

17. Measure and Monitor:

Regularly measure your website's performance metrics using tools like Google Analytics, and set up alerts to monitor performance regressions.

By implementing these performance optimization techniques and continuously monitoring your website's performance, you can ensure that your web applications load quickly and provide an excellent user experience, regardless of the device or network conditions. Performance optimization is an ongoing process that should be part of your web development workflow.

9.3 Web Security Basics

Web security is of paramount importance in today's digital landscape. Ensuring the security of your web applications and websites protects sensitive user data, maintains trust, and prevents potential threats. In this section, we'll explore the fundamental concepts and best practices for web security.

1. HTTPS and SSL/TLS:

Always use HTTPS to encrypt data transmitted between the user's browser and your server. Implement SSL/TLS certificates to secure connections and protect against eavesdropping.

2. Input Validation:

Validate and sanitize all user inputs to prevent SQL injection, cross-site scripting (XSS), and other injection attacks. Use parameterized queries for database interactions.

3. Authentication and Authorization:

Implement strong user authentication mechanisms, including password hashing and salting. Use role-based access control (RBAC) to restrict user access to specific resources.

4. Session Management:

Securely manage user sessions with techniques like secure cookies, session timeouts, and proper handling of session data. Be cautious with storing sensitive information in client-side storage.

5. Cross-Site Request Forgery (CSRF) Protection:

Implement anti-CSRF tokens to prevent attackers from tricking users into performing unintended actions on your site.

6. Content Security Policy (CSP):

Utilize CSP headers to mitigate XSS attacks by specifying which sources of content are allowed to be executed on your web pages.

7. Security Headers:

Implement security-related HTTP headers, such as X-Content-Type-Options, X-Frame-Options, and X-XSS-Protection, to enhance the security of your web application.

8. Secure File Uploads:

If your application allows file uploads, validate file types, use unique file names, and store uploaded files outside the webroot to prevent execution of malicious scripts.

9. Error Handling:

Avoid exposing detailed error messages to users. Log errors securely and provide generic error messages to users.

10. Security Testing:

Regularly perform security testing, including vulnerability scanning and penetration testing, to identify and remediate potential security weaknesses.

11. Security Patching:

Keep all software components (e.g., web server, libraries, frameworks) up to date to patch known vulnerabilities.

12. Content Security:

Be cautious about the content you embed from external sources. Always validate and sanitize user-generated content, and avoid unnecessary third-party scripts.

13. Data Backups:

Regularly back up your data, and test the restoration process to ensure data recovery in case of data loss or security incidents.

14. Security Education:

Train your development and operational teams on security best practices. Promote a security-aware culture within your organization.

15. Incident Response Plan:

Develop an incident response plan to effectively address security breaches and minimize their impact.

16. Compliance with Regulations:

Adhere to relevant data protection regulations, such as GDPR or HIPAA, depending on your geographic location and the nature of your application.

17. Continuous Monitoring:

Implement continuous security monitoring to detect and respond to security threats in real time.

Web security is an ongoing process that requires vigilance and adaptation to evolving threats. By following these web security basics and staying informed about the latest security trends, you can significantly reduce the risk of security incidents and protect your users and data.

9.4 Accessibility Guidelines

Ensuring web accessibility is not only a legal requirement in many regions but also a fundamental aspect of good web development practice. Web accessibility ensures that people with disabilities can perceive, understand, navigate, and interact with your web content effectively. In this section, we'll explore essential accessibility guidelines and best practices.

1. Semantic HTML:

Use semantic HTML elements to structure your content correctly. For example, use `<nav>` for navigation menus, `<button>` for interactive buttons, and `<h1>` to `<h6>` for headings.

2. Keyboard Navigation:

Ensure that all interactive elements, including forms and buttons, can be accessed and operated using a keyboard alone. Test your website's navigation flow with the "Tab" key.

3. Focus Management:

Make sure that the focus indicator is visible and prominent when navigating with a keyboard. Users should always know where their keyboard focus is on the page.

4. Alt Text for Images:

Provide descriptive alternative text (`alt` attributes) for images to convey their content and function to screen readers. Decorative images should have empty `alt` attributes (alt="").

5. Captions and Transcripts:

Include captions for videos and transcripts for audio content. Ensure that media players are accessible and provide controls for adjusting volume and playback speed.

6. ARIA Roles and Attributes:

Use ARIA (Accessible Rich Internet Applications) roles and attributes to enhance the accessibility of dynamic and interactive elements like modal dialogs, sliders, and accordions.

7. Proper Heading Structure:

Organize content with a logical and hierarchical heading structure. Avoid skipping heading levels, and ensure that headings accurately describe the content that follows.

8. Color Contrast:

Ensure sufficient color contrast between text and background to make content readable for users with visual impairments. Tools like WCAG color contrast checkers can help.

9. Form Accessibility:

Make forms accessible with descriptive labels, error messages, and clear instructions. Provide helpful hints and suggestions for required input formats.

10. Responsive Design:

Ensure that your website is responsive and adapts to various screen sizes and orientations. Test with different viewport sizes and assistive technologies.

11. Testing with Screen Readers:

Test your website with popular screen readers like JAWS, NVDA, or VoiceOver to identify and address accessibility issues. Familiarize yourself with screen reader keyboard shortcuts.

12. User Testing:

Include people with disabilities in usability testing to gather real-world feedback and identify potential accessibility barriers.

13. Document Accessibility:

Provide accessible PDFs and other documents when offering downloadable content. Ensure text is selectable, and images have alt text within documents.

14. A11Y Resources:

Stay informed about web accessibility standards and guidelines, such as WCAG (Web Content Accessibility Guidelines). Refer to authoritative resources like WAI (Web Accessibility Initiative).

15. Continuous Education:

Keep learning and staying updated about evolving accessibility practices and technologies. Attend web accessibility conferences and webinars.

16. Compliance and Legal Obligations:

Understand the legal requirements for web accessibility in your region, such as Section 508 in the U.S. and the EU Web Accessibility Directive.

17. Accessibility Statement:

Publish an accessibility statement on your website, outlining your commitment to accessibility and how users can request assistance or report accessibility issues.

Web accessibility is an ongoing process that requires dedication and a commitment to inclusive design. By following these accessibility guidelines, you can create web content that is usable and enjoyable for all users, regardless of their abilities or disabilities.

9.5 Keeping Up with Web Development Trends

In the fast-paced world of web development, staying up-to-date with the latest trends, tools, and technologies is essential to remain competitive and deliver high-quality projects. In this section, we'll explore effective strategies for keeping up with web development trends.

1. Continuous Learning:

Web development is an ever-evolving field. Dedicate time to learning new technologies and techniques regularly. Consider online courses, tutorials, and workshops on platforms like Coursera, Udemy, or freeCodeCamp.

2. Follow Industry Blogs and News:

Subscribe to web development blogs and news websites to receive updates on the latest trends, best practices, and emerging technologies. Popular sources include Smashing Magazine, CSS-Tricks, and A List Apart.

3. Attend Conferences and Meetups:

Participating in web development conferences and local meetups is an excellent way to network with professionals, gain insights, and learn about emerging trends firsthand. Look for events like Google I/O, GitHub Universe, and local tech meetups.

4. Join Online Communities:

Engage with web development communities on platforms like Stack Overflow, GitHub, Reddit, and dev.to. Participate in discussions, ask questions, and share your knowledge.

5. Experiment with New Technologies:

Don't be afraid to experiment with new languages, frameworks, and libraries. Create small projects to test your understanding and gain practical experience.

6. Read Books:

Books can provide in-depth knowledge and insights into specific web development topics. Look for books on JavaScript, CSS, and web performance optimization, among others.

7. Follow Thought Leaders:

Follow influential figures in the web development industry on social media platforms like Twitter and LinkedIn. They often share valuable resources, tips, and insights.

8. GitHub and Open Source:

Contribute to open-source projects on GitHub. This not only helps you gain experience but also exposes you to the latest coding practices and collaboration tools.

9. Online Courses and Bootcamps:

Enroll in online courses and coding bootcamps that offer comprehensive web development curricula. These programs often include hands-on projects and guidance from experienced instructors.

10. Podcasts:

Listen to web development podcasts during your commute or free time. Podcasts like "ShopTalk Show" and "Syntax" cover various web development topics.

11. Code Challenges and Hackathons:

Participate in coding challenges on platforms like LeetCode and HackerRank. Join hackathons to collaborate on real projects and expand your skill set.

12. Tech News Aggregators:

Use tech news aggregators like Hacker News and Techmeme to stay informed about the latest industry news and discussions.

13. RSS Feeds:

Set up an RSS feed reader to consolidate content from your favorite blogs and news sources. This allows you to efficiently scan headlines and choose articles of interest.

14. Explore Emerging Technologies:

Stay curious about emerging technologies like Progressive Web Apps (PWAs), WebAssembly, and WebRTC. Experiment with them in personal projects.

15. Mentorship:

Consider finding a mentor or becoming a mentor yourself. Mentorship relationships can provide valuable guidance and insights.

Remember that web development is a vast field, and you don't need to master everything. Focus on areas that align with your interests and career goals. By consistently learning and adapting to new trends, you'll keep your web development skills sharp and relevant.

CHAPTER X
Beyond the Basics: What's Next?

10.1 Exploring Advanced JavaScript and Frameworks

JavaScript is a versatile and powerful programming language used for web development. In this section, we'll delve into advanced JavaScript concepts and explore popular JavaScript frameworks that can take your web development skills to the next level.

1. Advanced JavaScript Concepts:

- **Closures:** Understand how closures work and their practical applications in JavaScript.

- **Promises and Async/Await:** Learn about asynchronous programming in JavaScript, using promises and the async/await syntax.

- **Prototypes and Classes:** Explore JavaScript's prototype-based inheritance and modern class syntax.

- **Functional Programming:** Dive into functional programming concepts like higher-order functions and immutability.

- **ES6+ Features:** Familiarize yourself with the latest ECMAScript features, such as destructuring, spread/rest operators, and template literals.

2. JavaScript Frameworks:

- **React:** Explore the React library for building user interfaces. Learn about components, state management with Redux or Context API, and routing with React Router.

- **Angular:** Discover Angular, a comprehensive framework for building robust web applications. Understand modules, components, services, and dependency injection.

- **Vue.js:** Learn Vue.js, a progressive JavaScript framework. Explore Vue components, directives, and Vue Router for building dynamic applications.

- **Node.js:** Extend your JavaScript skills to the server-side with Node.js. Explore the event-driven, non-blocking I/O model, and build RESTful APIs with Express.js.

- **Express.js:** Dive deeper into Express.js to create RESTful APIs and learn about middleware, routing, and database integration.

- **Webpack:** Explore Webpack for bundling and optimizing JavaScript, CSS, and assets in your projects.

- **TypeScript:** Learn TypeScript, a statically typed superset of JavaScript, to catch errors early and enhance code quality.

- **Testing Frameworks:** Discover testing frameworks like Jest, Mocha, and Jasmine to ensure the reliability of your JavaScript code.

- **GraphQL:** Explore GraphQL for efficient data querying and manipulation in web applications.

3. Building Real Projects:

Apply your knowledge by building real-world projects using advanced JavaScript and frameworks. Consider creating a dynamic web application, a single-page application (SPA), or a full-stack application that combines both frontend and backend technologies.

4. Continuous Learning:

Stay updated with the evolving JavaScript ecosystem by regularly following blogs, tutorials, and documentation related to the frameworks and technologies you're interested in.

5. Open Source Contributions:

Contribute to open-source projects related to JavaScript and its frameworks. This can provide valuable experience and help you collaborate with other developers.

6. Online Courses and Bootcamps:

Enroll in advanced JavaScript courses or bootcamps to deepen your understanding and receive structured guidance.

By exploring advanced JavaScript concepts and frameworks, you'll be well-equipped to tackle complex web development projects and stay competitive in the ever-changing field of web development. Continuously honing your skills and adapting to new technologies will be essential for your success.

10.2 Backend Development and Server-Side Programming

Backend development is a crucial aspect of web development that deals with the server-side of web applications. In this section, we will explore the fundamentals of backend development, server-side programming languages, and technologies commonly used in building robust web applications.

1. What is Backend Development?

Backend development refers to the server-side logic of a web application. It involves handling requests from the frontend, processing data, interacting with databases, and sending responses to the client.

2. Server-Side Programming Languages:

Backend development can be done using various programming languages. Here are some popular choices:

- **Node.js:** Node.js is a runtime environment that allows you to run JavaScript on the server. It's known for its non-blocking, event-driven architecture and is commonly used with frameworks like Express.js.

- **Python:** Python is a versatile language often used for web development. Frameworks like Django and Flask make it easy to build powerful web applications.

- **Ruby:** Ruby, combined with the Ruby on Rails framework, offers a productive environment for building web applications.

- **Java:** Java is a widely used language for backend development, particularly in enterprise-level applications. Java-based frameworks like Spring Boot are popular choices.

- **PHP:** PHP has been a longtime favorite for web development, especially for building dynamic web pages. Frameworks like Laravel provide modern PHP development capabilities.

3. Key Backend Concepts:

- **APIs (Application Programming Interfaces):** Understand how to create APIs to enable communication between the frontend and backend. RESTful APIs and GraphQL are common approaches.

- **Databases:** Learn about database management systems (DBMS) like MySQL, PostgreSQL, MongoDB, and how to interact with them from the backend.

- **Authentication and Authorization:** Implement user authentication and authorization mechanisms to secure your web applications.

- **Server Deployment:** Explore options for deploying your backend code, including cloud platforms like AWS, Azure, or Heroku.

4. Building a Backend Project:

- Consider building a simple backend project, such as a RESTful API or a content management system (CMS), to apply your knowledge.

5. Testing and Debugging:

- Explore testing frameworks and best practices for ensuring the reliability of your backend code.

6. Scalability and Performance:

- Learn about scaling strategies and optimizing backend code and database queries for better performance.

7. Security:

- Understand security best practices to protect your backend from common vulnerabilities like SQL injection, cross-site scripting (XSS), and more.

8. Version Control:

- Use version control systems like Git to manage your backend code and collaborate with other developers.

Backend development is a vast field with numerous technologies and practices to explore. By mastering the essentials of backend development and server-side programming, you'll have the skills to create powerful and secure web applications that can handle real-world demands.

Continuously expanding your knowledge and staying up-to-date with the latest trends is essential for success in this field.

10.3 Database Integration

Database integration is a critical aspect of web development that allows you to store, retrieve, and manage data for your web applications. In this section, we will explore the fundamentals of database integration, types of databases, and how to work with databases in web development.

1. Introduction to Database Integration:

   - **Databases** are organized collections of structured data used to store and retrieve information efficiently.

   - **Database Management Systems (DBMS)** are software applications that enable you to interact with databases. Common DBMS options include MySQL, PostgreSQL, MongoDB, and SQLite.

2. Types of Databases:

   - **Relational Databases:** These databases use tables with rows and columns to store data. Examples include MySQL, PostgreSQL, and Microsoft SQL Server.

   - **NoSQL Databases:** These databases use a flexible schema and can store unstructured or semi-structured data. Examples include MongoDB and Cassandra.

   - **In-Memory Databases:** These databases store data in system memory, providing ultra-fast data retrieval. Examples include Redis and Memcached.

3. Working with Databases in Web Development:

   - **Database Design:** Understand the importance of designing your database schema correctly to efficiently store and retrieve data.

   - **CRUD Operations:** Learn how to perform CRUD (Create, Read, Update, Delete) operations on your database.

   - **Database Connectivity:** Use programming languages like Python, JavaScript, or PHP to connect to databases and execute queries.

   - **ORM (Object-Relational Mapping):** Explore ORM frameworks like Sequelize for Node.js, Django ORM for Python, or Hibernate for Java to simplify database interactions.

4. Data Modeling and Schema Design:

   - Understand the process of designing the structure of your database tables, including defining relationships, constraints, and indexes.

5. Securing Databases:

   - Implement security measures such as authentication, authorization, and encryption to protect your database from unauthorized access and data breaches.

6. Handling Large Data Sets:

- Learn techniques for optimizing database performance when dealing with large volumes of data.

7. Real-World Examples:

- Explore practical examples of integrating databases into web applications, such as creating a blog platform or an e-commerce website.

8. Database Deployment:

- Consider different hosting and deployment options for databases, including cloud-based solutions like Amazon RDS, Azure SQL Database, or self-hosted databases.

9. NoSQL Databases and Beyond:

- Gain insights into when and why to choose NoSQL databases for specific use cases.

Database integration is a crucial skill for web developers, as most web applications rely on data to function effectively. By understanding database fundamentals, designing efficient schemas, and mastering the tools and technologies for working with databases, you can build robust and data-driven web applications.

10.4 Building Web Applications

In this section, we will delve into the process of building web applications, taking you through the essential steps, technologies, and best practices involved. By the end, you'll have a comprehensive understanding of how to create dynamic and interactive web applications.

1. Planning Your Web Application:

  - **Define Your Goals:** Clearly outline the objectives and purpose of your web application. Determine what problems it will solve and for whom.

  - **User Stories and Wireframing:** Create user stories to understand how users will interact with your app. Develop wireframes and mockups to visualize the user interface.

2. Choosing the Right Technology Stack:

  - **Frontend Technologies:** Decide on frontend frameworks and libraries, such as React, Angular, or Vue.js, to create the user interface.

  - **Backend Technologies:** Choose a backend technology like Node.js, Ruby on Rails, Django, or Express.js to handle server-side logic and database interactions.

  - **Database:** Select an appropriate database system based on your application's needs, whether it's a relational database like MySQL or a NoSQL database like MongoDB.

- Hosting and Deployment: Explore hosting options like AWS, Heroku, or Vercel for deploying your web application.

3. Building the Frontend:

- HTML/CSS: Create the structure and style of your web pages using HTML for content and CSS for layout and design.

- JavaScript: Implement interactivity and dynamic behavior using JavaScript. Understand the DOM (Document Object Model) to manipulate web page elements.

- Frontend Frameworks: If you've chosen a frontend framework, develop components and views to build your application's user interface.

4. Implementing the Backend:

- Server Setup: Set up your backend server, configure routes, and handle HTTP requests and responses.

- Database Integration: Connect your application to the database, define schemas, and create models for data storage.

- Authentication and Authorization: Implement user authentication and authorization to secure your application's resources.

- API Development: Create RESTful or GraphQL APIs for frontend-backend communication.

5. Testing and Debugging:

- **Unit Testing**: Write unit tests for individual components to ensure they work as expected.

- **Integration Testing**: Test how different parts of your application work together.

- **Debugging:** Learn effective debugging techniques to identify and fix issues.

6. User Experience and Accessibility:

- **Responsive Design:** Ensure your web application is accessible on various devices and screen sizes.

- **Accessibility (A11y):** Implement accessibility best practices to make your app usable by all, including people with disabilities.

7. Deployment and Scaling:

- **Deployment:** Deploy your web application to a hosting platform, configure servers, and set up continuous integration and deployment (CI/CD) pipelines.

- **Scaling:** Plan for scalability by optimizing database queries, caching, and load balancing.

8. Maintenance and Updates:

- **Regular Maintenance:** Keep your application up to date with security patches and bug fixes.

- **Feature Updates:** Continuously improve your app by adding new features based on user feedback.

Building web applications is a dynamic process that involves frontend and backend development, database integration, and ensuring a great user experience. By following best practices and staying updated with the latest web development trends, you can create web applications that meet user needs and stand the test of time.

10.5 A Glimpse into the Future of Web Development

The field of web development is constantly evolving, driven by technological advancements and changing user expectations. In this section, we will explore emerging trends and technologies that provide a glimpse into the future of web development.

1. Progressive Web Apps (PWAs): PWAs are web applications that provide a native app-like experience on the web. They work offline, offer fast loading times, and can be installed on a user's device. Implementing PWAs is becoming more common, as they improve user engagement and retention.

2. WebAssembly (Wasm): WebAssembly is a binary instruction format that enables high-performance execution of code in web browsers. It allows developers to run code written in languages like C, C++, and Rust directly in the browser, opening up new possibilities for web applications.

3. Single Page Applications (SPAs): SPAs, such as those built with React, Angular, or Vue.js, are gaining popularity due to their smooth user experiences and reduced server loads. They load a single HTML page and dynamically update content as users interact with the app.

4. Serverless Architecture: Serverless computing allows developers to focus on writing code without managing server infrastructure. Services like AWS Lambda and Azure Functions enable the automatic scaling of applications based on demand.

5. Artificial Intelligence (AI) and Machine Learning (ML): AI and ML are increasingly integrated into web applications to provide personalized experiences, automate tasks, and make data-driven decisions.

6. Web 3.0 and Blockchain: The concept of Web 3.0 envisions a decentralized internet powered by blockchain technology. It aims to give users more control over their data and online identities.

7. Augmented Reality (AR) and Virtual Reality (VR): AR and VR are finding their way into web development, offering immersive experiences for users. Web-based AR and VR applications are accessible through browsers, eliminating the need for specialized hardware or apps.

8. WebAssembly (Wasm): WebAssembly is a binary instruction format that enables high-performance execution of code in web browsers. It allows developers to run code written in languages like C, C++, and Rust directly in the browser, opening up new possibilities for web applications.

9. API-First Development: Building APIs before developing frontend or backend components is becoming a common practice. This approach streamlines development and enables multiple platforms (web, mobile, IoT) to interact with the same data.

10. Voice Interfaces and Chatbots: Voice-controlled interfaces and chatbots are enhancing user interactions. Integrating natural language processing (NLP) into web applications enables voice search and chatbot-driven customer support.

11. Cybersecurity and Privacy: With increasing concerns about online security and privacy, web developers will need to focus on implementing robust security measures, including encryption, authentication, and data protection.

12. Web Sustainability: Sustainability in web development involves optimizing websites for energy efficiency and reducing their carbon footprint. Developers are exploring ways to make the web more eco-friendly.

13. Web3 and Decentralization: The Web3 movement aims to create a decentralized internet where users have more control over their data and online interactions. Blockchain technology plays a significant role in this vision.

14. 3D Graphics and WebXR: 3D graphics and WebXR (Extended Reality) are transforming web experiences. They enable immersive 3D content and virtual reality experiences directly in web browsers.

15. Continual Learning: Staying current with the latest web development trends, tools, and frameworks will be essential for web developers. Online courses, tutorials, and developer communities are valuable resources for ongoing learning.

As you look ahead to the future of web development, embracing these trends and technologies can help you stay competitive and create innovative web applications that meet the needs of tomorrow's users. Web development is a dynamic field, and staying informed and adaptable is key to success.

Appendix A
HTML and CSS Reference

HTML Elements and Attributes

In this HTML and CSS reference, we'll explore the essential HTML elements and attributes that are commonly used in web development. HTML (Hypertext Markup Language) is the backbone of web pages, defining the structure and content, while CSS (Cascading Style Sheets) is used to control the presentation and styling of those elements.

HTML Elements:

HTML elements are the building blocks of web pages. They consist of tags that enclose content and provide structure to the document. Here are some fundamental HTML elements:

1. `<html>`: The root element that wraps the entire HTML document.

2. `<head>`: Contains metadata about the document, such as the page title and links to stylesheets and scripts.

3. `<meta>`: Provides metadata like character encoding and viewport settings.

4. `<link>`: Links to external resources like stylesheets.

5. `<script>`: Embeds JavaScript code or references external scripts.

6. `<body>`: Contains the visible content of the web page.

7. `<div>`: A generic container used for grouping and styling elements.

8. `<p>`: Represents a paragraph of text.

9. `<a>`: Creates hyperlinks to other web pages or resources.

10. `<img>`: Embeds images in the document.

11. `<ul>` and `<ol>`: Create unordered and ordered lists, respectively.

12. `<li>`: Represents list items within `<ul>` or `<ol>`.

13. `<table>`: Defines a table structure.

14. `<tr>`, `<th>`, and `<td>`: Table row, table header cell, and table data cell elements, respectively.

15. `<form>`: Creates a form for user input.

16. `<input>`: Represents input fields for forms.

17. `<textarea>`: Provides a multi-line text input field.

18. `<button>`: Creates clickable buttons.

19. `<h1>` to `<h6>`: Define headings of decreasing importance.

HTML Attributes:

HTML elements can have attributes that provide additional information or modify their behavior. Some common attributes include:

1. `class` and `id`: Used for styling and JavaScript interactions.

2. `src`: Specifies the source URL for elements like images and scripts.

3. `href`: Specifies the target URL for hyperlinks.

4. `alt`: Provides alternative text for images (useful for accessibility).

5. `width` and `height`: Define the dimensions of images.

6. `type`: Specifies the type of input in form elements.

7. `value`: Sets the initial value for form elements.

8. `placeholder`: Provides a hint or example text for form inputs.

9. `disabled`: Disables user interaction with an element.

10. `required`: Requires that a form field be filled out before submission.

Example:

```html
<!DOCTYPE html>
<html>
<head>
  <title>My Web Page</title>
  <link rel="stylesheet" href="styles.css">
</head>
<body>
  <h1>Welcome to My Website</h1>
  <p>This is a simple example of HTML content.</p>
  <a href="https://www.example.com">Visit Example.com</a>
  <img src="image.jpg" alt="An example image">
  <ul>
    <li>Item 1</li>
    <li>Item 2</li>
  </ul>
  <form>
    <label for="name">Name:</label>
    <input type="text" id="name" name="name" required>
    <button type="submit">Submit</button>
  </form>
</body>
```

```
</html>
```
```

Understanding HTML elements and attributes is fundamental for web development. They provide the structure and interactivity needed to create engaging and functional web pages. As you continue your journey in web development, mastering these elements and attributes will be crucial.
```

Common CSS Properties and Values

In this CSS reference, we'll explore some of the most commonly used CSS properties and their values. CSS (Cascading Style Sheets) is a stylesheet language used to control the layout and presentation of web documents. Understanding these properties and values is essential for styling web pages effectively.

1. Color Properties:

- `color`: Sets the text color.

- `background-color`: Defines the background color.

- `border-color`: Specifies the border color.

Example:
```css
h1 {
    color: blue;
    background-color: yellow;
    border-color: red;
}
```

2. Typography:

- `font-family`: Specifies the font for text.

- `font-size`: Sets the size of the font.

- `font-weight`: Defines the font thickness (e.g., bold).

- `line-height`: Sets the space between lines of text.

- `text-align`: Aligns text left, right, center, or justified.

- `text-decoration`: Adds decorations like underline or strikethrough.

Example:

```css
p {
    font-family: Arial, sans-serif;
    font-size: 16px;
    font-weight: bold;
    line-height: 1.5;
    text-align: center;
    text-decoration: underline;
}
```

3. Layout:

- `width` and `height`: Sets the dimensions of elements.

- `margin` and `padding`: Defines spacing around elements.

- `display`: Specifies how an element is displayed (e.g., block, inline).

- `position`: Controls the positioning of an element.

- `float`: Allows elements to float next to each other.

Example:

```css
.container {
    width: 80%;
    margin: 0 auto;
    padding: 20px;
    display: flex;
    position: relative;
    float: left;
}
```

4. Backgrounds:

- `background-image`: Sets a background image.

- `background-repeat`: Controls image repetition.

- `background-size`: Defines image sizing.

- `background-position`: Sets the position of the background image.

Example:

```css
.hero-section {
    background-image: url('background.jpg');
```

background-repeat: no-repeat;

background-size: cover;

background-position: center center;

}

```

## 5. Box Model:

- `border`: Sets the border properties.

- `border-radius`: Adds rounded corners.

- `box-shadow`: Applies shadows to elements.

Example:

```css
.box {
    border: 2px solid #333;
    border-radius: 10px;
    box-shadow: 5px 5px 10px rgba(0, 0, 0, 0.2);
}
```

6. Transitions and Animations:

- `transition`: Adds smooth transitions on property changes.

- `animation`: Creates animations using keyframes.
```

Example:

```css
.button {
    background-color: blue;
    color: white;
    transition: background-color 0.3s ease;
}

.button:hover {
    background-color: red;
}
```

These are just a few of the common CSS properties and values used in web development. CSS provides a powerful way to style and layout web pages, and mastering these properties will help you create visually appealing and responsive designs. Remember that CSS is highly customizable, and you can combine properties to achieve the desired visual effects.

Appendix B
JavaScript Reference

JavaScript Objects and Methods

In this JavaScript reference, we will delve into common JavaScript objects and methods that are essential for web development. JavaScript is a versatile programming language used for creating dynamic and interactive web applications. Understanding these objects and methods is crucial for harnessing the full power of JavaScript.

1. String Object:

- `.length`: Returns the length of a string.

- `.charAt()`: Retrieves a character at a specified position.

- `.concat()`: Combines two or more strings.

- `.toUpperCase()` and `.toLowerCase()`: Converts text to uppercase or lowercase.

Example:

```javascript
var text = "Hello, World!";
var length = text.length; // 13
var firstChar = text.charAt(0); // 'H'
var combined = text.concat(" Welcome!"); // "Hello, World! Welcome!"
var upperCaseText = text.toUpperCase(); // "HELLO, WORLD!"
```

```
```

2. Array Object:

- `.length`: Returns the length of an array.

- `.push()`: Adds elements to the end of an array.

- `.pop()`: Removes the last element from an array.

- `.join()`: Converts an array into a string.

- `.forEach()`: Executes a function for each array element.

Example:

```javascript
var fruits = ["apple", "banana", "cherry"];
var length = fruits.length; // 3
fruits.push("orange");
fruits.pop();
var fruitString = fruits.join(", "); // "apple, banana, cherry"
fruits.forEach(function (fruit) {
    console.log(fruit);
});
```

3. Date Object:

- `new Date()`: Creates a Date object.

- `.getFullYear()`, `.getMonth()`, `.getDate()`: Retrieves date components.

- `.getHours()`, `.getMinutes()`, `.getSeconds()`: Retrieves time components.

- `.toDateString()`, `.toTimeString()`: Converts to date and time strings.

Example:

```javascript
var currentDate = new Date();

var year = currentDate.getFullYear();

var month = currentDate.getMonth();

var day = currentDate.getDate();

var hours = currentDate.getHours();

var minutes = currentDate.getMinutes();

var dateStr = currentDate.toDateString(); // "Sat Oct 01 2023"

var timeStr = currentDate.toTimeString(); // "14:30:00 GMT+0000 (Coordinated Universal Time)"
```

4. Math Object:

- `.random()`: Generates a random number between 0 (inclusive) and 1 (exclusive).
- `.floor()`, `.ceil()`, `.round()`: Rounds numbers down, up, or to the nearest integer.
- `.max()` and `.min()`: Returns the maximum or minimum value from a list of numbers.

Example:

```javascript
var randomNumber = Math.random(); // Random value between 0 and 1

var roundedNumber = Math.round(2.7); // 3

var maxNumber = Math.max(5, 10, 3); // 10
```

```
```

These are some of the fundamental JavaScript objects and methods you'll frequently encounter in web development. JavaScript's rich ecosystem of objects and functions enables you to build dynamic and interactive web applications. By mastering these basics, you'll be well-equipped to work with more advanced JavaScript concepts and libraries.

Common JavaScript Events

In this JavaScript reference, we will explore common JavaScript events. Events are actions or occurrences that happen in the browser, such as a user clicking a button or resizing the browser window. JavaScript allows you to capture and respond to these events, enhancing the interactivity and functionality of web applications.

1. Click Event:

- The `click` event occurs when a user clicks on an HTML element, such as a button or a link.

- Example:

```javascript
var button = document.getElementById("myButton");

button.addEventListener("click", function() {

    alert("Button clicked!");

});
```

2. Mouseover and Mouseout Events:

- The `mouseover` event triggers when the mouse pointer enters an element, and `mouseout` triggers when it leaves.

- Example:

```javascript
var element = document.getElementById("myElement");

element.addEventListener("mouseover", function() {

    element.style.backgroundColor = "red";
```

```javascript
});
element.addEventListener("mouseout", function() {
    element.style.backgroundColor = "white";
});
```

3. Keydown and Keypress Events:

- The `keydown` event occurs when a key is pressed down, and `keypress` occurs when a key is pressed and released.

- Example:

```javascript
document.addEventListener("keydown", function(event) {
    if (event.key === "Enter") {
        alert("Enter key pressed!");
    }
});
```

4. Submit Event:

- The `submit` event is triggered when a form is submitted, typically by pressing Enter or clicking a submit button.

- Example:

```javascript
var form = document.getElementById("myForm");
```

```javascript
form.addEventListener("submit", function(event) {

    event.preventDefault(); // Prevents the default form submission

    alert("Form submitted!");

});
```

5. Window Resize Event:

- The `resize` event occurs when the browser window is resized.

- Example:

```javascript
window.addEventListener("resize", function() {

    console.log("Window resized");

});
```

6. Load Event:

- The `load` event occurs when an HTML page or an external resource (e.g., an image) finishes loading.

- Example:

```javascript
window.addEventListener("load", function() {

    alert("Page loaded!");

});
```

These are just a few examples of common JavaScript events that you can utilize to create responsive and interactive web applications. Events play a crucial role in web development, enabling you to respond to user actions and create dynamic user experiences. Understanding how to use events effectively is a fundamental skill for web developers.

Glossary

Key Terms and Definitions

In this glossary, we will define key terms and concepts related to web development, HTML, CSS, JavaScript, and other relevant topics. Understanding these terms is essential for becoming proficient in web development.

1. HTML (Hypertext Markup Language): HTML is the standard markup language used to create web pages. It consists of elements that define the structure and content of a web page.

2. CSS (Cascading Style Sheets): CSS is a style sheet language used to describe the presentation and layout of HTML documents. It allows you to control the appearance of web pages.

3. JavaScript: JavaScript is a versatile and widely-used programming language for web development. It enables interactive and dynamic web page behavior.

4. DOM (Document Object Model): The DOM is a programming interface for web documents. It represents the structure of a web page and allows you to interact with it programmatically.

5. HTTP (Hypertext Transfer Protocol): HTTP is the protocol used for transferring data over the World Wide Web. It defines how requests and responses should be formatted.

6. API (Application Programming Interface): An API is a set of rules and protocols that allows different software applications to communicate with each other. Web APIs enable web services and data exchange.

7. Responsive Web Design: Responsive web design is an approach to web development that makes web pages render well on a variety of devices and window or screen sizes.

8. Front-End Development: Front-end development involves creating the user interface and user experience of a website or web application. It typically includes HTML, CSS, and JavaScript development.

9. Back-End Development: Back-end development involves building and maintaining server-side components of web applications. It includes server scripting, database management, and server configuration.

10. Full-Stack Developer: A full-stack developer is proficient in both front-end and back-end web development, allowing them to work on all aspects of web applications.

11. Responsive Images: These are images that adapt to different screen sizes and resolutions to ensure optimal viewing on various devices.

12. SEO (Search Engine Optimization): SEO is the practice of optimizing web content to improve its visibility and ranking on search engine results pages (e.g., Google).

13. Framework: A framework is a pre-built, reusable set of tools, libraries, and conventions that simplifies and standardizes web development tasks.

14. Git: Git is a distributed version control system used for tracking changes in source code during development.

15. HTTPS (Hypertext Transfer Protocol Secure): HTTPS is the secure version of HTTP, ensuring encrypted communication between a web browser and a web server.

16. Cookie: A cookie is a small piece of data stored on a user's device that is sent back to the web server with each subsequent request. It is often used for user authentication and tracking.

17. Web Hosting: Web hosting is a service that allows individuals and organizations to make their websites accessible on the internet.

18. Debugging: Debugging is the process of identifying and fixing errors or bugs in software code.

19. Responsive Design: Responsive design refers to the practice of creating websites that adapt and provide an optimal viewing experience across different devices and screen sizes.

20. User Interface (UI): UI encompasses all the elements and components that users interact with on a website or application.

21. User Experience (UX): UX focuses on the overall experience and satisfaction of users when interacting with a website or application.

22. URL (Uniform Resource Locator): A URL is a web address that specifies the location of a resource on the internet.

23. Semantic HTML: Semantic HTML refers to using HTML elements that convey the meaning and structure of the content, improving accessibility and SEO.

24. Cross-Browser Compatibility: Cross-browser compatibility ensures that a website functions correctly on various web browsers, such as Chrome, Firefox, and Safari.

25. Cache: Cache stores frequently accessed data to reduce load times and improve website performance.

This glossary provides definitions for essential terms in web development. Familiarity with these concepts is crucial for anyone working in the field of web development.

CONCLUSION

In this comprehensive guide, we've embarked on an exciting journey through the world of web development. From the foundational principles of HTML, CSS, and JavaScript to advanced topics like responsive design, web security, and emerging technologies, we've covered a wide spectrum of knowledge to help you become a proficient web developer.

Throughout this book, we've strived to provide clear explanations, practical examples, and step-by-step guidance to empower you on your web development endeavors. We've explored the intricacies of building responsive and interactive web pages, understanding the Document Object Model (DOM), and mastering the art of modern web design.

You've learned about the importance of clean and maintainable code, performance optimization, and web security best practices. We've delved into the world of back-end development, databases, and web application architecture. Additionally, we've peered into the future of web development, offering insights into emerging trends and technologies that will shape the industry.

As you continue your web development journey, remember that learning is an ongoing process. Technology evolves, and staying up-to-date with the latest developments and trends is essential. Whether you're building personal projects, launching websites for clients, or pursuing a career in web development, the knowledge and skills you've gained here will be valuable assets.

Thank you for choosing this book as your guide to web development. We hope it has been a valuable resource in your quest to become a proficient web developer. Your commitment to learning and growth is commendable, and we wish you every success in your future endeavors in the exciting and ever-evolving field of web development.

If you have any questions, feedback, or need further assistance, please don't hesitate to reach out. We're here to support you on your journey.

Best wishes,